A Perfect Creation

A Perfect Creation

The Light
behind the
Dark Side of *Genesis*

Robert E. Joyce

LifeCom

Published by

LifeCom

St. Cloud, Minnesota, USA

ISBN   978-0-615-25155-4

For information, address *LifeCom*, Box 1832, St. Cloud, MN 56302

Contents

Preface

The present brief treatise offers a new dimension to the traditional theist worldview. The book contains a supposition and hypothesis for believers to mull over seriously and not to write off as something already considered and rejected. It is not Origenism. It is not Gnosticism. It is a new way of understanding Christian Revelation, accessible to any serious seeker of truth. This understanding is new in theological exposition, but not in the truth of Revelation.

No new doctrine is suggested. But there would seem to be an increase in depth perception, like going from 2D vision to 3D on the same truths, particularly creation and the origin of evil.

There is a similarity in the history of art. At one time, painters seemed to be unable to give three-dimensional renditions. Later, a breakthrough occurred in the manner of painting and many were able to fashion three-dimensional looking figures and scenery even on flat surfaces. Analogously, we are long overdue for an ontological movement in Faith-consciousness enabling greater depth-perspective on the meaning of Revelation and reason.

I am totally committed to the Catholic Faith in dogma and morals. The presentation of new theory is an attempt to deepen and enhance understanding of that Faith and of what is perennially true in Christianity. Jewish theists and others, too, might find some reasons for reworking their own theology.

*****

I am particularly grateful for the contemporary insights into the philosophy of being by Thomistic philosophers, such as Jacques Maritain and Etienne Gilson. They and others have been creatively faithful to the masterful integration of faith and reason developed by St. Thomas Aquinas through unique insight into the meaning of *being*.

Thomistic philosophers generally have seen the need to ground themselves in the perspective of Aquinas on the relation of essence to being (*esse*). The present work suggests something more about this time-honored distinction.

In any event, people who philosophize in the context of faith need to refrain from trying to escape basic Thomistic philosophy, with its roots in common and uncommon sense.

Tragically, however, many have become addicted to the texts and to the logic of a kind of "peeping Thomism." We need to go into, through, and beyond the metaphysics of St. Thomas, even as he did with respect to Aristotle, Plato, Augustine, and others.

St. Thomas was a *truth*ist, not a Thomist. Renewal will come from the roots of Faith that are ever the same, yet ever more deeply known, philosophically and theologically.

A Perfect Creation: The Light behind the Dark Side of Genesis is an initial attempt to help us face our personal and communal "dark sides" and to admit more of the infinite Light that loved us immediately and perfectly "into" *being*. There is more to follow, including a large volume, *When God Said Be, We Said Maybe: An Inside Story of the Creation, the Crash, and the Recovery.*

The present introduction to creation *out of nothing* and to the origin of evil is intended to evoke response, positive and negative. Comments and questions are most welcome through postal or email messages. I look forward to your reaction or response.

This book is written in the firm belief that, contrary to perhaps one's first reading, every point developed is in accord with the *Magisterium* of the Catholic Church, to which I am committed for life.

Finally, I give thanks to Mary Rosera Joyce, my spouse and fellow philosopher. She has been a steady support with assistance in writing and with significant ideas, such as the dynamics of ontological insight, the poverty of the "rational animal" definition, and the concept of energy as passive-reactive. We have been married in life and in thought for almost 50 years. We rejoice together in God's gifts of faith and reason.

Robert E. Joyce, Ph.D.
Professor Emeritus
St. John's University
Collegeville, Minnesota
Website: www.Lifemeaning.com
Email: robertjoyce@charter.net

Chapter 1

Introduction to a New Theistic View

The music is loud and clear coming from those who believe in Adam and Eve. We are absorbed in our victimization by our first parents. We think their sin in Eden started it *all*. Somehow we *had* to inherit *their* sin. They botched our inherited human nature and we became captives of this nature, and thereby were necessarily conceived in sin.

In light of this pervasive interpretation, let us face some questions that the music seems to have drowned out. If our first parents had not sinned, what might have become of us? How would we be relating to God right now? Would we have been able to be born in this world without pain and suffering and to be taken into eternal life without death?

If Adam and Eve had not inflicted us with a human nature damaged by sin, what then? Could some subsequent parents have afflicted us with a sin of their own anyway? Is human nature essentially like an animal species, where the individuals are totally subordinate to the nature* and

behavior of all others of their kind? Is personal freedom*
not so personal after all? And not so free?[1]

Apparently, the background drums of space and time
have damaged our hearing so much that we think God *had*
to create us as progeny of Adam and Eve. Space and
time—the measures of passive matter* and motion as well
as of opaque matter itself—are regarded as being
necessary to the life of a *human* person. In other words, if
we did not have matter in a spatiotemporal form, we
would not be human; we would be angels.

This assumption, however, is absurd. We are obsessed
with knowing* things *only* or *mainly* in terms of space and
time. But our most essential powers are not material.
There is no space for intellect and will. They are spaceless
and timeless in themselves.

The activities of intellect and will cannot be known by
any kind of sensation. So, we need to move more securely
into another way of knowing, a way that truly *transcends,
but includes,* space and time and sensory knowledge—
without being conditioned by them, even in part.

As it is now, we are conflicted. We believe that our
inheritance of Adam's sin is not at all our *personal* fault
(though it is somehow personal to us). But we assume that
God could not create us to be ourselves and to be the kind
of being* we are, without making us subject to cosmic
conditions. We fail to see what being created *out of
nothing* really means.

---

[1] A term that is found in the Glossary is followed by an *asterisk*, on the *first*
instance of its usage. The Glossary is structured topically and can be read as a
whole. Or terms can be consulted briefly, as they are encountered in the main
body of the book.

Creation *ex nihilo** (*out of nothing*) had to be a perfect creation. God was the *only* agent or doer. This infinitely perfect act of *gifting* being to created persons (angelic and human) necessarily resulted in perfect beings (persons) who are perfectly free to respond perfectly. So, we must exist here and now in space and time because *we failed to act perfectly* with our perfect, beingful freedom of response. As God said *BE*, we immediately and freely said *maybe*.

If we had not originatively committed this *personal original sin*, there would have been for us no space and time—the *inherently imperfect* measures of the fallen world. A *perfect* space and time are, like a square circle, *impossible*.

It is immensely passive to think that we, *as creatures of matter and motion*, come *directly* "from the hand of God." We fail our very personhood in believing such. We impede our ability to see, as persons, who we are and who we are not; and we severely hamper our ability to love intimately and freely. We are self-trapped in a fixation on space-time conditions that are only a small, if important, *part* of our *fallen* human way of knowing and thinking.

The Forest and the Trees

Our earthly predicament, as in Plato's story of the Cave, is both a tragedy and a comedy.

Here we are, living like the prisoners depicted in the story. The shadows that we are viewing include all objects of direct, immediate consciousness*—the whole sensible world of matter and motion.

Also involved are the objects of indirect or reflective consciousness: ideas and meanings that come from the spontaneous exercise of our ability to be conscious *of* our consciousness of things. Meanings and values are gleaned in that reflective way.

But our ideas and attitudes also arise from a suppressed and mainly repressed* realm of human intellection. They result from subconscious and even unconscious* *knowing*.

We are living ever in denial. We cannot see what really *is—just as it is*—because of our fixation on its shadows. We refuse to turn around, as it were, in order to confront our outcast nature that keeps us looking away from the light, rather than into it.

Because we exist in a fallen condition, we cannot sustain looking directly at reality as gifted by God. Not only is it sin-affected, but also sin-*effected*. We blame our plight basically on Adam and Eve. We claim that their offense at the origin of *history*—not the same as at the origin of our *being*—weakened us in mind and will.

In blaming Adam and Eve *alone*, however, for our inheritance of a damaged human nature, we are somewhat right, and also quite wrong.

There is a personal reason *why* each of us inherited the sin of Adam and Eve; and *why* we all "die in Adam" (1 *Corinth.* 15:22). The reason must be because we all *sinned with* Adam. God's infinite goodness and infinite power *cannot* force upon us the sin of another person.

So, while it might be true to say that all have sinned *in Adam*, because all die in Adam, it is truer to say that all have sinned both *with* and *in* Adam. We are not fallen *only* because of Adam's fall; we are members of "Adam's fallen race," because of our *originative* sin,* done together with Adam—causing the need for *redemptive* creation, along with space and time and the dust from which Adam's recovery began to be fashioned.

The mammoth reason *why* we inherited Adam's wounded nature is just this. We must have sinned *originatively*, causing ourselves to be susceptible to eventual membership in the *fallen* human community. Uniquely and personally, we failed to respond fully, at the moment of being gifted with our be-ing, *out of nothing*, by the creating act of God.

Since this originative sin was not temporal or spatial, we cannot *remember* it. *Genesis* does not report it. The creation stories of *Genesis* tell *directly* of our *redemptive* creation—our subsequent creation, one that was *ex aliquo*, out of a void, dust, a rib—*not* out of *nothing*. *Genesis presupposes* an act of weak reception of being on our part—an act that is ontologically (not temporally) prior to the episodes in Eden.

Genesis is also about creation *ex nihilo*, but indirectly and symbolically so. The *light* of originative creation (*ex nihilo*)—underlying and embracing the remedial creation of *Genesis*—is like a glow above the trees in a thick forest. We are attentively fixed, as it were, on the thickets of trees, bushes, and all manner of vegetation on the forest floor. As a result, we do not realize directly the glowing radiance. And yet that is the illumination that makes our sight even possible, well beyond any light given by a "bonfire"—by acts of virtue and sin in this world.

We live on the planet earth in the cosmos today and we think of how it all got started. From cosmologists to biologists and paleontologists, we hear of physical formations having vast temporal parameters. Causes for *becoming** are discussed aplenty.

But little appreciation is given to the *being* of the becoming itself. Not how did conditions A cause conditions B, but how did the whole succession of conditions occur in the first place? And why are they there?

Not, who *made* us (out of something)? But, who brought us into being (out of nothing)? The same God doing different, though co-relatable, creations.

We are so absorbed by the *creation of becoming* that we neglect to appreciate the *creation of being*. Becoming eclipses being. The creation in *Genesis* serves to hide the creation *ex nihilo*, in the light of which *Genesis* would make preeminently better sense.

We cannot see the forest for the trees. We cannot see *being* for all the *becoming* (the coming and going of physical, mental, moral, emotional, and spiritual states). Yet everything that is becoming is *being*, even though not everything that is *being* is becoming. (God and the angels, for instance, are not *in process* at all.)

On the one hand, we are enamored of the "trees." They are constituted by everyday events, as well as historical ones, such as those we read about in Scripture, including the details of *Genesis*. And our devotion to a linear logic— one that lacks a serious allowance for paradox—keeps us trapped in the "trees."

On the other hand, the "forest" itself is our prime predicament in the face of infinite Love. God's *ex nihilo* creation is an *inter*personal one, absolutely requiring a free, immediate, and personal response from each person—whether angelic or human. God is not a super Artisan or Craftsman working on dead matter.

God is infinitely personal and originatively creates persons and persons *only*. By a *protoconscious** act of free willingness, at the durationless moment of our creation *out of nothing*, we must have caused the *need* for our *becoming.* We must have done something bad to our being. God, infinite goodness and infinite power, surely did not.

We need to realize that our *be*-ing is an act that *we* are *doing*, and with which we were gifted *ex nihilo.* By our first *act* of *be*-ing, we willed to *be-come* less than who we are by trying to *be* more than who we are. Our *personal* response to the gift of *being*—to the *perfect creation—caused* the need for the existence of the whole passivity-based world, our present habitation.

In an immediate, divine response to our hesitation to be who we are, God began to create redemptively, *within* timelessness, what we know as time. And, in a divine activity, God unconditionally identified with us by taking on our human nature in order to free us from our sin. This redemptive activity was effected and revealed in 'the fullness of time.'

One of the questions marking our concern about the *original* sin* in Eden is *whether* we—as well as Adam and Eve—could have been personally responsible for an *originative sin* that the Bible does not proclaim directly. May we reasonably infer from what we do know about human nature and Scriptural Revelation that this unique kind of trangression occurred in a spaceless, timeless manner, and that we have *spiritually repressed* it and are now, for a variety of reasons, unaware of committing it?

Would an acknowledgement of such an originative sin render richer the whole of Christian belief in particular—and the whole of theistic belief in general—without taking away the mystery of good and evil, creation and the fall? Would it help us to participate more deeply in the mystery of creation, sin, and redemption and deepen the roots of what we have been taught to believe? My answer is *yes,* but I desire *yours,* after serious consideration.

Right from the start, I will stress the importance of belief in God's *infinite* goodness and *infinite* power, and our God-like human freedom. Keeping our minds and hearts immersed in these few basic truths perennially common to most theists, we can now explore some of their deeper meanings in light of the Faith-hypothesis of *personal responsibility for originative sin.*

In explicating the new perspective, we will have to use originally temporal terms for realities that are not at all durational, such as the *moment* of creation out of nothing, the *moment* of decision at death,* and so forth. And some readers will be fiercely dedicated to using linear logic to critique these theses. The typical logic lock will prevent them from seeing the *being* of it all. Yet, as Einstein once said in another context, "No problem can be solved from the same level of consciousness that created it. "

Knowing by the heart, as well as by the mind, is necessary. Not by the sentimental mind and heart, but by the *core* of the intellect and *will.* We might have to admit an awesome truth that Sacred Scripture never denies, ever implies, and quietly summons from the depths of our being.

Chapter 2

From Chaos to Cosmos

The *Book of Genesis* begins by referring to a void, an emptiness, even a chaos (*Genesis* 1:2). Darkness reigned. Only then do we begin to read of the light, the firmament, plants, animals, and human beings.

Why did God start by creating heaven and earth with a void? Or why is there a gap between the first two verses of the text? Did the first sentence declare implicitly that God created heaven and earth perfect? Such would be impossible. Earth is inherently imperfect. The matter of the whole cosmos is basically passive.

So, it is likely that this first declaration of *Genesis* ("In the beginning, God created...") was a generalization about a second or rehabilitative creation. Such a "creation for recovery" would involve a condition of darkness that is actually mentioned in *Genesis* and definitely bespeaks imperfection.

From this beginning there was something lacking. Something that could not come solely from God. A first or originative creation was not explicitly noted, but such would have resulted in perfect creatures, since it was simply an act of God alone—of unlimited goodness and unlimited power.

The second or "rehab creation" caused the cosmos. It was a *process*—whether it took six days or six eons. Space and time were required. But every process, as well as space and time, is inherently imperfect, involving passive matter and motion. All things therein are not just doing or acting, but are being done *to*, and eventually being "done in." This planetary cosmos, then, is not simply the result of an infinite Being, effecting something totally fresh and perfect *out of nothing*.

Creation *out of nothing* is solely the activity of God. No one cooperated with God in the *doing* of *that* act. The *act* had to be infinite, as all of God's acts are, and had to *result in* effects that are complete finite perfection* of being and freedom: *an immaculate creation** of perfect persons with the perfect *ability* to respond as they willed.

The results of the creating act, however, depicted in the first chapter of *Genesis*, were not perfect beings. Yet they were created by God, who is both *infinitely* good and *infinitely* powerful. And so, we must wonder why the effects of God's act were not perfect?

Genesis, for instance, could be the story of redemption, of a cosmos, created out of *something*—out of a mess that needed to recover. But surely it is not the result of God's immediate act of creating *out of nothing*. The void, the darkness—as well as the dawning light—came, at least partly, from a perfect finite base that had somehow fallen into imperfection. This redemptive creation was not *out of nothing* (*ex nihilo*), but *out of something* (*ex aliquo*). What was this chaos, this "something"?

In the first lines of Scriptural Revelation, the *reality* of a void might be taken as merely figurative and symbolic, or simply literal in every way, or by some combination of the two kinds of meaning. Still, in order to understand how the emptiness or even chaos got there in creation, we have to be sure about the *infinity* of God. The wasteland—whether symbolic or literal—could not have come *solely* by the act of a truly infinite being.

In an unconscious effort of avoidance, perhaps, many thinkers throughout the ages have regarded the *Genesis* story of creation as "just the way it was." They think that God willed creation to be, at its beginning, quite imperfect and in need of 'cultivation.' God, then, is regarded practically as *finite*, even though we sometimes use the word *infinite*. This subtle, but momentous, mistake in the theology about what is being revealed has amounted to "the case of the missing infinity."

Despite this disparity, many Christians claim to know, through faith in Christ mediated by his Church, that *original sin*—not originative sin—is inherited historically and that all people suffer from its *real* guilt that must be forgiven or removed if they are to be eligible for entry into a Godly everlasting life. Christians believe that all human beings on earth inherit this sin from Adam and Eve and that it entails a primordial weakness and proneness toward "actual sin," right within human nature as existing in the space-time world.

Besides, Christians claim to know, in part, *how* it occurred. It entailed an act of freely chosen disobedience to God's express command. It did not occur as a surprise burden placed by an infinitely just God upon the first ill-choosing couple. Adam and Eve were *personally* guilty. We also know that a "third party" was involved: the evil one, the deceiver, adding a profoundly social dimension to this kind of personal disobedience.

Nevertheless, these truths and others about the *what* and the *how* of *original sin* leave us free to find new interpretations of their implications. We are privileged to be able to participate in the discovery of the origins of our existence in space and time, *and* in be-ing itself.

The stories of creation in *Genesis* are filled with details like a forest of trees. But we are dimly aware of a muted light behind the actual accounts. We rarely, if ever, attend to this light. And, if we were to do so, we might attain a kind of three-dimensional understanding of the revelation in *Genesis* and in the whole of Sacred Scripture. But, alas, for the most part, we develop interpretations already in place.

What, then, is the basic background or *being*ground for the void and chaos at which believers stare as the Bible opens in *Genesis* One? And can we see more vividly and clearly the light behind this dark side?

Chapter 3

The Missing Infinity of God

As we have been taught to read the *Holy Bible*, we are left to wonder whether God is *infinite*. We *say*, "God is really infinite." But do we *mean* it? In the Hebrew Testament, and even somewhat in the Christian Testament, many of the accounts make God seem quite finite and reactive.

Most believers in God might say, nonetheless, that God is truly infinite. Yet many would qualify their claim. They might think that God is infinitely good, but not infinitely powerful. God, they surmise, cannot really stop innocent children from suffering some of the worst torments.

But, if God is infinite Being, then infinite power is *necessarily* involved. God is *both* unlimited goodness *and* unlimited power: *unlimited actuality*.

In the history of thought, there seems to be hardly any consistent development of the notion of infinity. After all, it is quite difficult for flawed finite persons to conceive of *infinite Personhood*.

To our spatialized minds, infinity often seems to be an impersonal trait. In the field of mathematics, for instance, we postulate a kind of "infinity." Yet, there is no such thing. So-called "mathematical infinity" is an impersonal "infinity," better regarded as *indefiniteness*—not real, qualitative, ontological (beingful) infinity.

In the Eastern world, pantheism is quite widespread. The "everything is god" mentality tries to compensate unconsciously for the lack of awareness of real infinity. In each form of pantheism, the lack of understanding genuine transcendence fosters a false sense of divine immanence. The essences of both infinite and finite being are conflated, for all practical purposes, into the notion of an indeterminate, *non-personal* Self. With a rare exception or two, the strains of Hinduism and Taoism present an *impersonal* kind of Absolute. And Buddhism requires agnosticism.

In Western thought, the transcendent infinity of divinity is known only with great difficulty. Greek philosophers, such as Plato, tended to think that the divine was finite and that the infinite was something that applied to the imperfect realms of reality. Earlier philosophers had a quite material notion of infinity. Anaximander, Leucippus, and Democritus had their own versions. The latent "atomism" behind modern and contemporary science bears the perennial burden of confusion over the indefinite, the indeterminate, and the infinite.

Even in the theistic tradition, both East and West, the record is muddled. Bright spots of illumination, however, include attempts by Gregory of Nyssa and others to know that God is infinite. Augustine struggled. Then, many centuries later, came the articulations by Thomas Aquinas and others.

But even among the followers of St. Thomas there have been unwitting substitutes for infinity that have made it difficult to face God's unique *kind* of power and unique *kind* of goodness. Some contemporary Thomists, for instance, have avoided using the concept of God's infinity when developing the meaning of the being of creatures as "participation."

Many practitioners of metaphysics refer to God as the "fullness of Being." That makes it sound as if there were a void to fill. And they are also inclined to think of created persons as participants in the "fullness." This egregious mistake obfuscates the true infinity of God, who is infinitely *within* (not inside) us and infinitely *different from* (not distant from) us. Created persons "participate" in God's infinite Being, but they do so finitely and relationally. They do not "take part" in the Godhead. They are not "partly infinite." The infinite is not the fullness of the finite. There is nothing *full* about the unlimited kind of being.

In order to articulate the idea of created participation in God's Being, some seem to think that the idea of God as the *fullness* of Being fits better than the idea of God as *infinite* or *unlimited* Being. But this leads to confusion, because fullness definitely implies finitude.

Whenever created persons are conceived as "taking part in" God's Being, the notion of infinity takes a back seat. We know that created beings are not infinite in being, and so we play around with the quasi-quantitative terminology of fullness. Fullness, however, cannot really mean infinite, because there is a proper meaning for finite ontological, qualitative fullness.

Is it a Defect to be a Creature?

The practice of shying away from the infinity of God reveals a major problem. God is said to be the fullness of Being—perfect in being—without specifying necessarily that God is *infinitely* perfect. God cannot be the Being that is merely perfect. God is the Being that is *unlimitedly perfect*.

Jesus even *urged us* to be perfect, just as our heavenly Father is perfect (*Matt.* 5:48). He obviously meant for us to be finitely perfect, even as our Father is infinitely perfect. There is no conflict between finite perfection and infinite perfection. But there is an impossible conflict in a finite being striving to be infinite or in "borrowing a bit of the being" of God. God's unlimited being is not on loan.

So, we might ask again, does the Supreme Being really have a fullness? If God is truly infinite, there is no question of a fullness. Fullness is only proper to something with limits that can be filled "to the brim," as it were, to make it *full. Only a finite being can be full.*

Moreover, it would seem to be, at least, semi-pantheistic to think that God has the fullness of the pure perfections that are found in creatures. Created persons have or, rather, *are* their *own* perfections. These qualities are *like* God's, but they are finite.

Created intellects,* for instance, always attain *finitely* the truth about both finite and infinite being. They cannot infinitely attain truth about anything. Created wills, for instance, always unite finitely with goodness, even with unlimited goodness. And finite beings are capable of the fullness of perceiving beauty finitely, even in the presence of infinite beauty. But one need not be infinite in order to know and love the infinite.

The difference between finite goodness and infinite goodness is…well, infinite. Not some quasi-difference in "infinite quantity," but a real, infinite difference in quality.

Surely, there is a radical difference between the two kinds of perfection. God *cannot be* the fullness of created, limited perfection "and still be God." *Unlimited* perfection has *no possible* "fullness." God does not "fulfill us," but gives us the power for our own fulfillment through *full union with* divine Being.

Infinite perfections are not the same *kind* as the perfections that are finite. Infinite goodness, for instance, is qualitatively different from finite goodness; it is the kind of goodness that *causes* the *being* of finite goodness. God's ways are *not like* our *finite* ways, even though our ways ought to be quite *like* God's *infinite* ways. Paradoxically, we are both like and unlike the divine Being.

Nonetheless, we human knowers inveterately think of God as a "fullness" of what we know as finite perfection. We distinguish created persons from God. But we then portray them as lacking a fullness of their own and as inherently *un*full or imperfect in *their* being. In this way, the distinction between God and creatures pivots around fullness and unfullness rather than around infinite and finite—an entirely different distinction.

Being then begins to sound like a very subtle kind of quantitative whole, of which there can be only one (univocal) fullness. The so-conceived divine "fullness" is played off against created fullness and the latter comes out as somehow defective. The *two different kinds* of perfection—infinite and finite—are not given proper recognition.

It is one thing to *relate* and to *contrast* the finite and the infinite. But it is quite another to *compare* them. When the ill-conceived "infinite fullness" or the properly conceived infinite perfection of uncreated being is somehow assumed to be the *measure* of the created person's finite fullness, the latter obviously comes up woefully lacking.

Created persons, however, do not *lack* even a whit of divine perfection or "fullness." Unlimited Being ought not to be the standard for created being. Because creatures are not at all infinite, they do not "have" *anything* of "infinite quality." There is no basis for comparison, such as calling God's truth and goodness the *maximum* in truth and goodness. There is *no maximum* to infinite truth and goodness. Nonetheless, there is a superabundant basis for acknowledging interrelationship between the uncreated and the created.

Finite perfection has its own maximum: the perfect finite quality of being as it emanates freely from God's infinite act of creating the finite being itself. The perfect fulfillment for created, received being is *not* the infinite being of the Giver, but the *perfect finite being* of the gift *as gifted by* that infinite Gifter.

We fail to recognize the infinite *difference* (not distance) between the created person and the uncreated, infinite Being. This omission keeps us treating God as a mega-creature. At best, God is known weakly as an infinite Gifter, or, in many instances, not really known as infinite.

Chapter 4

The **Interpersonal** Act of Creating

Many philosophers and theologians seem to avoid unwittingly the real infinity of God by characterizing created persons as inherently lacking in *being*. But this concept amounts to a caricature of creation. All created *persons* are the immediate result of God's infinitely powerful act of loving them perfectly "into" being. Each of them is *necessarily* a perfect, unique likeness of God.

Subpersonal creatures, of course, *are actually defective in being*, because they are without intellect and will—without powers to know and to receive themselves and others. Does this mean that the infinitely good and powerful Being can *directly create out of nothing* these defective or imperfect beings?

God *cannot* do so, and "still be infinite." Subpersonal or imperfect beings are not directly created by God, but are created indirectly, by way of a spatiotemporal process. Ultimately, all created reality is effected by God. But only persons—complete beings—are created *directly out of nothing* with the complete *ability* to respond positively, negatively, or, in the case of humans, hesitantly.

Somehow many people seem to have the idea that a given reality can be created imperfect out of nothing and then attain perfection by the activity of God. But not even God can effect perfection *out* *of* what would be *originatively* imperfect. In anything that is *originally and essentially* imperfect, there is no potency—whether active or passive potency—for perfection.

On the one hand, out of the imperfect can only come the less imperfect, never the perfect. The growth of a tree from seed to maturity would seem to be development from the imperfect to the less imperfect or "more fulfilled." But a perfect tree can never be.

On the other hand, the imperfect *can* come from the perfect, where the perfect is a person, having complete freedom to determine personal destiny. Failing in the first act of freedom, the perfect person becomes imperfect. This self-rendered imperfection of being cannot be rendered perfect without Someone who is unlimitedly perfect actually doing the critical work of salvation. The imperfect can, so to say, come from the perfect; but the perfect can never come *from* the "pristinely imperfect."

This means that the direct creation of persons is an act of infinite *being*, creating perfect finite *beings*. At the moment of creation *out of nothing*, these person-beings simply *are*, as gifted.

Imperfect finite beings, however, are quite another matter. They do not simply *be*. They also *exist*. They stand outside themselves (*ex-sistere*) in their *manner* of being. Existence, then, is not the same as *being*. Exisence is a *defective kind* of being.

Theists are definitely inclined to overlook the *inter*personal character of the infinite act of creation, whereby the Creator creates, and every creature gives an immediate and free response to, the perfect gift of being.

Christians, for instance, have been bogged down in debates about the "making" of the physical universe. In the discussion of our origins, we never, or rarely, hear about the *inter*personal act of God, directly gifting persons to be with an *intrinsic, immediate response-ability.*

Both theistic evolutionists and creationists portray God as a rather impersonal Creator, who *makes* the world during a long or short period. They seem not even to suspect that, at the absolute moment of gifting them to be, God said, "Be," and every created person—angelic and human—gave an entirely free, immediate, interpersonal response to being created. A *personal* God does *everything* person-to-person. *Initially, nothing impersonal comes by the activity of God.*

For both theistic evolutionists and creationists, however, God works more like a human artisan, fashioning "out of a void or chaos" the various stages of creaturehood. Creation is regarded as a process. But, however long or short it may be—eons or mere days—a process is, at best, an activity of realities that are imperfect, attempting to become less imperfect.

Most folks start talking about our response to creation as though it were a be-*coming*, not a be-*ing*. But be-coming necessarily involves a process of one kind or another. And all process is a process *of* that which is *be*-ing. In order to become or come-to-be, a person must first *be*. There is no *coming*-to-be without someone *who* is there already *on the way*.

Even in matters of growth in physical nature itself, every *living* being comes to be all at once and then unfolds itself or becomes more differentiated. The whole being is there all at once—say, as a zygote—and then becomes increasingly differentiated. More beautiful, mature, and functional. Only artifacts and non-living things come to be or "become" gradually, part by part. They *are not* until the last "vital" part or piece is added. (A stool needs at least three legs; a chair needs four.)

Living things, however, are totally what they are from the start, and the "parts" gradually develop as the whole of the living being becomes more and more (functionally) what it already (naturally) is. A fertilized acorn, for instance, *is* an oak tree in its nature, though not yet in its functionality.

The Absolutely Originative Creation

Nonetheless, the absolutely originative creation by God had to be immediate and perfect and interpersonal. The act of creation was an *interpersonal* act of God gifting, *to each created person*, the fullness of perfect finite being. Every person was given perfect *freedom to receive actively and immediately* the unique gift of being.

This first freedom was not at all a passive potency* (an ability to be "done *to*"); it was an active potency*: a *purely active* ability to *do* the *be*-ing gift itself by saying fully and immediately *yes*.

Only the created person could *receive* and *do* his or her own *be*-ing. God could not *do* the *be*-ing of the creature *for* the creature; nor could any creature *do* the *be*-ing of any other. Each created person did his or her own *receiving* and *doing* of the gift, by the *immediate exercise of* that gift—receiving and giving self, person to Person, finite one to infinite One.

To be is to be *both* unique *and* interrelated. Even now, from the tiniest snowflake to the Triune God, every being is unique and not the same as *any* other. But every being is also *related* to *every* other being, without there being the slightest "exchange of identities." *This* snowflake cannot ever become *that* snowflake, no matter how it "looks."

God created beings who were utterly unique and totally related. The first, un-derivative creatures were simply *persons*—not subpersons. They were capable of receiving, with perfect intelligence and love, the gift of unique and relational being.

God created only unique beings who were perfectly able to create their own response; and they must have done so immediately and interpersonally. There was no delay at all. Even the slightest bit of duration would have meant that some passivity and imperfection were initially involved.

This perfect moment was the perfect interface. All created persons responded, well or poorly and in perfect freedom, to God's gift, who they were *gifted to be*. They were *not faced* with God's *glory*. This glory could enter them only upon their responding in freedom perfectly. But they knew *directly and perfectly* the infinite goodness and infinite love of their Gifter. They knew to Whom they were responding.

This absolutely originative knowing activity was done, even by human persons, with purely active powers of knowing and loving: agent intellect* and agent will,* now so obscure and immensely repressed. By these purely active powers—with no passivity at all—they could know being as being (both infinite and finite being) and could respond perfectly. By their very being, they knew their Creator to be infinite and themselves to be finite.[2]

---

[2] In the tradition of philosophy and theology, the agent intellect is portrayed generally as a light, but not as a knowing power. When we deny our part in originative sin, we inevitably accept the properties of knowing and loving only as they occur in this world that is the effect of sin. The idea of an agent *will* is

Some persons, like the good angels, must have said *fully yes* to being created. Others, like Lucifer and his cohorts, must have said *fully no*. Still others, indeed ourselves, must have said both *yes* and *no* (in effect, *maybe*).

These last thereby devastated, but did not totally destroy, their ability to receive fully—at least, in recovery—their own goodness and the glory of God.[3] They "hesitated" about reality and each said, in effect, "I am not sure I will to be finite, why can I not be infinite even as are the three Divine Persons who are gifting me to be." The demurral of these *maybe*-sayers was immediate and definite and utterly *free personally*, with no time or duration about it.

There was nothing passive about the beings—all persons—that God created *out of nothing*. They were all perfect kinds of unique being—angelic and human—with the perfect power to enter immediately and forever the infinite embrace of God. All were created as finite, unique likenesses of the infinite God: *able* to receive and to give, in perfect harmony, who and what they were. Each one was a unique, *finite, pure act of being*.

We *fallen* humans obviously failed to receive and give ourselves perfectly to God and to the whole of creation. Perhaps some of our originative *human* community of

---

virtually unknown and totally repressed by our religious and secular cultures. That *purely active* potency to *love* is the key power of our whole being in receiving ourselves as gift and receiving God as Gifter.

The agent intellect was not created to know in a passive-reactive way, nor was the agent will created to love in a passive-reactive way. That is the way they function now, under terms such as (passive) intellect and (passive) will. We need to exercise care in trying not to project how we know now onto our knowing and loving at the moment of creation *out of nothing*.

[3] Cf. *When God Said Be, We Said Maybe: An Inside Story of the Creation, the Crash, and the Recovery* by Robert E. Joyce (St. Cloud, MN: LifeCom, 2009). Many issues and aspects of this theme are given extensive treatment.

persons said *fully yes* and entered heaven immediately; perhaps some said *fully no* and fell to hell immediately. But we, who are the *maybe*-saying human persons, actively disabled ourselves from entering God's glory— hanging ourselves between heaven and hell.

Because of the *yes* in our *maybe*, we are able to hope for divine salvation. But because of the *no*, we are in great danger of everlasting ruin.

We remain perfect, as originatively gifted by God. But we are *also—in addition—imperfect*, as received by ourselves. Our imperfection is not simplistic imperfection, one that takes away perfection. It is a "dis-value added" imperfection—by virtue of our being *both* perfect (by God's gifting) *and* imperfect (by our deficient response).[4]

Self-Submerged and Spiritually Repressed

As an immediate result of our primal abuse of the power and freedom to love, we collapsed into a severely damaged condition of being.

Now, we are waking up in the remedial world of *be*-coming (our *be*-ing *coming* back to itself). We are called to repent of our primordial, personal, absolutely free plunge into selfishness. This *plunge* has been dubbed "the fall" by our spiritually repressed minds. We even blame it specifically on Adam and Eve.

---

[4] Physical, imperfect things lose their "original perfection" when they are broken or damaged. But they are not—as are spiritual realities— "flawless" at all to begin with. So, we can appreciate all physical beings as derivative and as elements of the redemptive universe only. Passively material things (subpersons) are intrinsically imperfect at all times, despite their relative goodness and beauty.

We *maybe*-sayers are imperfect by being *both* perfect *and* imperfect. We are not—like a broken vase or a dead tree—*imperfect both before and after the "breakage."* Physical things are imperfect intrinsically—with "parts outside of parts"—right from the start.

But the story of Adam and Eve is more than historically true. It is not only a report on the first *history*-making sin. The prime value of the account includes its symbolic meaning for each one of us. It is true that *with* Adam all have sinned. Adam is the head of the "fallen human race." But he is not the head of the originative community of human persons *ex nihilo*.

At the first, interpersonal, non-durational moment of being created ("out of nothing"), all created persons—angels and humans—were *gifted* with their being. We fallen humans poorly received—along with Adam and Eve and at least billions of their other eventual progeny—our unique and perfect beings. We effectively caused a division in our seamless selves: into a *yes* and a *no*—a *good side* and a *bad side,* a *light side* and a *dark side.* We all must have caused or created thereby—out of the perfect gift we *are*—the "tree of the knowledge of good and evil." That "Maybe Tree" became planted in the Garden of Eden, right in the face of our first parents themselves.

Adam and Eve represented all who needed recovery. They were tested not so much to see whether they would be faithful to the God who created them out of the dust (residue of the crash), but in order for them to awaken to their self-wrought weakened condition of being. God knew what they would do. It seemed to be a foregone conclusion when the Lord told Adam, "The day you eat of it, you shall die the death (*Genesis* 2:17)."

Original sin started the succession of multitudes of generated recoverers from *originative* sin. The fallen human community was being given the opportunity to attempt a "come back." God gifted them with the power to return to their originative selves through the ministry of the whole of the redemptive creation.

Originative sin, the supremely able, yet intentionally imperfect, *reception* of our be-ing was, in effect, our *willingness* to be *both* God-gifted *and* self-shifted. We received the gift by making a shift. We hesitated, as it were, to receive the gift of *being-infinitely-other-than-the-Giver*. As finite beings, we might have "compared" ourselves immediately to the infinite, and balked a bit, in effect, "wondering whether" we could have received, instead, an infinite being. We immediately evinced, with our perfectly active powers of intellect and will, a lack of responsive *be*-ing—a lack however slight or grave. Each one's response must have had its own characteristics and degree of *yes-no* (*maybe*).

The God-gifted *power* by which we did this was perfect. The *act* that *we* did with this power was imperfect. We exercised our perfect power imperfectly. The *power* did not *do* the act. *We* did. *With* the power.

This hesitation-to-be-who-we-are caused a self-rupture that must have largely obscured from ourselves who we are and who we could have been. As a result, we are now in a condition of almost totally functionalistic existence. We hardly know who we *are* and seem to be virtually unaware of our interpersonal, originative encounter with the infinitely loving God. We are nearly oblivious of our *self*-crashed condition and of the *originative* sin by which *all* of our weaknesses *ultimately* have come.[5]

The good will in our first act of freedom was impacted by our allowance of ill will at that same moment. Each of us might have said, "I do not know what it means to be

---

[5] We have not so much suppressed our originative sin as repressed it. The latter means we are unconsciously denying it. The former means we know it, but put it quickly out of mind.

Concerning the original sin of Adam and Eve, the origin of our personal evil came *through* this original sin, not only from it.

finite." Or something like, "Why am I finite? Why cannot I be infinite, too?" "Why cannot I be a 'fourth' Person of divinity?" Some *maybe*-sayers would have been more diffident than others.

By that free *protoconscious* act, we caused both the good effects and the bad.[6] The degree of *no*—even the slightest—to our own being and to God caused the collapse and the virtual obliteration of our awareness of the originative condition of being. The quality or degree of *yes* made it possible for our reclamation and potential salvation by God.

Participating in the world of space and time, we now have the opportunity to exercise our measure of functional freedom* on a limited and defective basis. And we are afforded the prospects of developing ever higher levels of functional freedom. But we are also far afield from our originally gifted state of being, wherein we had the *purely active* power to receive and to give—with no *passive* potency.

As the Evangelist Paul put it: "Eye has not seen nor ear heard nor has it entered into the human heart what God has prepared for those who love Him (1*Corinthians* 2:9)." In

---

[6] Protoconscious means the absolutely first act—one that "models" all the rest and is as fresh and pure as could be. This act was far more excellent in freedom and clarity than our most deliberate acts of freedom now in space and time. This protoconscious act of freedom was not strictly an alternative-choosing freedom, but was exercised at the very root of our being by our "freshly minted" agent intellect and agent will. (In our culture, the agent intellect, a great discovery of Aristotle, has been wrongly thought to be a non-knowing power. And the very existence or reality of an agent will seems to be historically a matter of almost total repression.)

Later, we will distinguish again the *act* from the *power* to act, including acts of agent intellect and agent will. The active powers of agent intellect and agent will must be understood to be working now with the passively responsive intellect and the passively responsive will,* wherein passive and active potency are interwoven.

our case, it was prepared, and we failed to receive it fully as gifted. We had the natural freedom* to express our essence perfectly. So, we are being exhorted in the work of redemption to receive gratefully the divine retrieval of our being by saying *yes* to redemption (and salvation) as fully as we can. If we refuse even that, we will ratify the *no* in our originative act of freedom.

We are in jeopardy of everlasting ruin. And we are still blaming Adam and Eve, even as they blamed the serpent, and the serpent blamed God. We are locked into the blame chain by playing the blame game, unwilling to recognize that we must have been created as perfect human persons with the perfect freedom to enter, immediately and forever, into ecstatic union with God. We do not even think of the *possibility* that we initially failed in *be*-ing. Our *spiritual* repression is more than massive. The history of thought and culture is rife with repression.

In the third century, however, Origen seemed to be intuiting our deeper responsibility when he proposed the idea of an existence prior to the present life—an existence in which we fell away from goodness and were subject to the world of space and in need of redemption (*De Principiis*). In the 19th Century, Julius Muller, a Lutheran theologian, developed what seemed to be a basic sense of personal responsibility for an original sin.[7] But such attempts to tell an "inside story" have been minimal compared to the justifications of the linear, relatively "outside story" of creation and the fall.

Origen and Muller, moreover, were not afforded the ontological leverage to see the interface of finite and infinite freedom. Origen, in effect, denied a decisive self-

---

[7] Muller, Julius. *The Christian Doctrine of Sin.* Edinburgh: T. & T. Clark London: Hamilton, Adams & Co., 1868.

determination for the created persons by seeming to teach a kind of universal salvation. Neither theologian seemed to recognize that the creation *ex nihilo* was an immaculate one, and that thereby all persons had the perfect freedom of self-destiny in love (or hate). Nor were they able to take into account the *spiritual repression* that was inexorably the immediate consequence of the originative, defective interpersonal encounter with God at creation. Systematic attention to the power of *unconscious* knowing began to find its advantage only in the 20th Century.[8]

Spiritual and emotional repression create an incalculable impact on our daily lives. Moreover, according to psychoanalytic theories, our defense mechanisms are many. But, curiously enough, some of the most effective defensive maneuvers at the preconscious* level—in the *spiritual* unconscious—have been the philosophical and theological attempts to portray *God's original creation of humans as involving passive potency.*

Perhaps the most absurd idea in the common theological *interpretation* of the Revelation of Scripture and Tradition

---

[8] Eric Fromm wrote about the power of dreams as the forgotten language. (*The Forgotten Language: An Introduction to the Understanding of Dreams, Fairy Tales and Myths*: New York: Rinehart & Co., Inc., 1951.) Peoples have always known that our unconscious speaks to us. But it is quite difficult to attend to it systematically.

A great stride toward full disclosure was taken by Jacques Maritain, who brought out the power of the spiritual unconscious: the preconscious area of knowing that is indigenous to creativity. His book, *Creative Intuition in Art and Poetry*, contains a fruitful analysis of the power of the agent intellect as "an illuminating sun of intelligibility." Maritain took some of his cues from the groundbreaking work of Sigmund Freud concerning the reality of the *psychological* unconscious—the emotional underbelly of everyday life.

I am claiming that the spiritual unconscious holds vast reaches of meaning at the depths of our being, wherein the originative, if partial, denial of our being occurred. The importance for human meaning at the level of *emotionally* unconscious drives (Freudian) is dwarfed by the impact of our *spiritual* drive to conceal from ourselves our first act of *be*-ing and *mean*-ing.

is the one that would claim, in effect, that God creates passive potency directly (*ex nihilo*). God is thought to have created the *passive* potencies found in trees and in angels, in water and in souls.

Our spiritual repression of *originative* sin makes it virtually impossible to see creation as an interpersonal act—solely God's act, necessarily inviting our immediate and most intimately personal response.[9]

---

[9] Our conscious kind of knowing, done in this world now, is a "focal point" for other kinds and levels of knowing, done "simultaneously." Our passively responsive intellects work away at knowing things consciously by the abstractive activities of simple apprehension, judgment, and reasoning. And these functional intellects "instinctively" suppress and repress ideas or meanings that then become "spiritually impacted" below the surface of consciousness.

But our *agent* intellects afford us the opportunity to *know* subconsciously, unconsciously, and above all protoconsciously. We know vastly more than we think we know. Knowledge is not only discovery, but also uncovery. And the latter's levels are many.

One problem with the traditional account of human knowing through external and internal sensory processes is that it tends to be an exclusivistic account, implicitly and heavily ruling out other simultaneous avenues of perception and intellection.

Chapter 5

How Our *Being* Fell into Existence

We have repressed our *originative* sin. We are living largely in denial. So, we are strongly inclined to overlook the critical difference between *exist-ing* and *be-ing*. We do not recognize what we have done to ourselves and to our freedom. Consequently, we take for granted the two kinds of *existence* in the cosmos, the subpersonal and the personal.

In the spatiotemporal world of our *conscious* knowing, there are at least two basic kinds of *existents*.

First, there are the subpersonal creatures: animals, plants, minerals, and the rest. They not only *are* or *be*; they also *exist*. Their *manner* of being is extrinsic or "outside themselves." They *ex*-ist. They "stand outside" themselves and one another (*ex-sistere*) by having parts: "parts outside of parts." They are created by God *ex aliquo* (out of something): out of the energy* and residue of the primal crash of multitudes of human persons at the moment of creation *ex nihilo*.

God's creation of these subpersonal existents prepared the way for the crashed human persons to make a comeback in what might be called the *redemptive* creation (creation *ex aliquo**), celebrated in the *Book of Genesis*. Such existents or excidents*—animals, plants, and inorganic substances—are expressions of subpersonal human *energy*. These part-beings are without intellect and will and are thus incomplete beings.

Our free response to creation *out of nothing* violated pristine human freedom. We thereby *caused* energy to exist by virtue of our self-trampled personal freedom. The explosion of our personal freedom caused collectively the disparate and fragmentive condition called cosmic matter and energy, now known as subpersonal being. The impersonal universe is, then, a formerly personal one, with which God works to bring about our recovery from the originative crash.

Second, there are the personal creatures, we ourselves, who originatively failed to will ourselves to be *fully* friends with God. We also *ex*-ist. We stand outside ourselves (*ex-sistere*). We are, as *Genesis* indicates, "cast out."

But the manner is striking. By our present mode of consciousness in earthly existence, we can allow ourselves to "look at ourselves" and to decide what we are going to do with our somewhat fragmentive selves. We are not just conscious of things, but are also conscious of our consciousness of things. And this reflective kind of consciousness, so dear to thinkers who are called existentialists, is the result of a distinctive "God-like," but distorted, freedom. We fallen humans both *are* and *exist*. We stand outside ourselves and one another—physically, emotionally, mentally, and spiritually.

God, however, and all created persons who are originatively without sin *do not exist*. They simply *are* or *be*. Unfortunately, philosophers and others often proceed merrily referring to the *existence* of God, rather than the *being* of God. Thereby they treat God and fully affirming created persons (the good angels, for instance) as on a par with sinful beings—beings that are "outside themselves within themselves." God is *unwittingly* regarded thereby as a supreme "cast out" kind of being. By such unconscious antics, we keep ourselves somewhat twisted in relationship to God. It is "convenient" because then we do not have to face what caused the twist and how it originated.

Originative Sin and Evolution

Because of the failure to distinguish existence from being, evolution is often confused with the original creation. Anyone who thinks, for instance, that God *originally* and *directly* created humans through evolution is denying who God is: infinitely perfect Being.

Evolution, however, is not creation *ex nihilo*. Like any *process*, evolution is inherently imperfect. At best, in any process the more developed is coming forth from the less developed. If it is real, then, evolution cannot be God's *perfect* activity of creating finite *being*.

The original act of creation is the infinite act of an infinite being. The created persons *resulting* from such an act must be immediately *perfect finite* beings—completely *able* to respond fully, freely, and immediately to the *gift that they are* and to the Gifter.

We need to honor God's *immaculate creation*: the immediate result of an infinitely powerful activity of creating *ex nihilo*. But if we are going to do so, we will have to acknowledge that this creating is absolutely perfect with perfect results as far as the *gifting* act is concerned. Evolution it is not.

If there is any truth at all to evolution, such a mega-process could only be part of *redemption*—the *ex aliquo* (out of *something*) recovery of fallen, self-deprived persons, who were originatively perfect in being and in freedom *ex nihilo*.

In a redemptive scenario, we could portray perfect, infinite Being as responding with redemptive intent and "working with" self-exiled creatures whose natural resistance to this responsive divine "working" is immense. Their resistance comes from a now-damaged, once perfect, finite freedom, with which they were initially endowed by God's creating them "out of nothing." At the moment of creation out of nothing, and *without any temptation at all*, they *received somewhat badly* the perfect gift that they *are*. To their perfect creation, they gave an imperfect reception.

Perhaps we could say that God gifted them *"out of nothing"* with perfect being and freedom, but they immediately and freely balked. Such reluctance to be finite in the face of *infinite* goodness necessarily caused them to crash. So, they are now struggling from the consequences of depriving themselves of immediate and perfect fulfillment.

These fallen human persons, by even the slightest withdrawal from *infinite* truth and beauty, would have severely disabled themselves. They would find themselves now in the process of being redeemed or reclaimed, after having badly exercised their first free act of receiving their being.

They are we. We were perfect as *gifted* by God, but imperfect and self-defective as *received* by ourselves *in that same first (non-temporal) moment*.

So, we now find ourselves imperfect. But we are not *simply* imperfect, as are plants and animals. We fallen persons are imperfect by being *both* perfect *and* imperfect. We imperfect person-beings retain our originatively God-endowed *perfect* being, but encumber it with our own willful imperfections of matter and of spirit.

Evolution, understood properly, could be *part* of our recovery from a massive malfunction of our originative perfectly-free, created personhood.

Passivity Passes for Receptivity

A prime example of overlooking the *infinite act of perfect creation* can be found in Aquinas' doctrine of being. St. Thomas teaches that even angels are composites of act and *passive* potency, right within their own being.

Their act of *be*-ing is thought to be necessarily limited by passive potency (their essence*): by the *essential* ability to *be done to*—to be determined not just by self, but by others. Every created person (angelic and human) is regarded as essentially *both* active *and* passive in *being*. Implicitly, God's perfectly good spiritual creatures are thought to be set in a spiritual S-R (stimulus-response) state of being.

So, for instance, when we say we are praying to a blessed angel, we think of the angel as being stimulated, affected, even tweaked, and *set upon by* our imprecation: that our prayer *does something to* the angel. And then the angel responds—positively or negatively. We overlook the power of an angel's being-*with* us, without being "done to" *by* us.

For Aquinas, no created person is *fully* self-determining. In the ability to receive the being that one is, no one is a pure (finite) act of *being*—and of *doing*.

In this manner, created persons are considered not merely as essentially finite beings, but as essentially passive beings as well—essentially defective. Apparently, God creates beings that are necessarily imperfect.

According to the theory, only God can be Pure Act. But that might be because all reality is being conceived as a kind of mega-finite whole—a "whole" of actualities with passive potentialities. This "whole" includes, of course, one "exception": necessarily pure actuality, the unmoved mover or uncaused cause. In this conceptualization, then, "pure actuality" is the basic way to distinguish God from creatures, each of which holds some degree of structural passive potency.

"Actuality and passive potentiality," however, are serving poorly for what should be the relevant difference between God and created persons: infinite, pure *actuality* and finite, pure *actuality*. The Thomistic "passivity viewpoint," affords no realization that God—at the moment of creation "out of nothing"—*must have created only persons, all of whom were perfect beings with perfect freedom*. In Scholastic discourse, the passivity that is natural to the present world has been directly—if unconsciously—applied *unreasonably* to the conditions of pristine creation.

There seems to be awareness that God was free to create or not to create-at-all. But another assumption seems inevitable: God was "free" to create "out of nothing" imperfect beings, because, it is thought, at least implicitly, that the effects of *any* cause—even of the Uncreated Cause—are necessarily imperfect. That was the way it was thought, *even if it was not said* that way. The effect was regarded as *necessarily* dependent on the cause, *especially* on the Uncreated Being of the Creator.

To the contrary, while retaining some of the basic meaning for "potency and act," we can say that God must have gifted—originatively—all created being with *purely active potency only,* and with *no passive potency* at all. Created persons were gifted with the purely active ability *to do*, to say *fully yes* to God and to the gift of their own being. They were not created with any ability *to be done to* (passive potency), or to be affected by others. They were super-related to all other created persons, and were able to relate-*with* all others, without being (passively) affected by them.

Only the created persons themselves could *make themselves* passive and imperfect in being. Each could *make self passive* by actively, but lamely, expressing God's gift to them. Each was able to impair the *purely active potency to receive perfectly their (uniquely finite) being*.

And so, multitudes of us did *fail* to receive *fully* our own beings at the originative moment of creation. Virtually all humans of space and time, with the rarest of exceptions (who are known only through divine Revelation), said less than fully *yes*.

Moreover, we seem to be either unaware of, or we do not care about, *perfect human* persons, who might well have said, in perfect freedom, fully *yes* at the moment of creation. *Thereby* they would have immediately entered beatitude, without need for redemption or for becoming (under Adam) members of the *fallen* human community.

In the *immaculate creation*, our God-gifted receptivity (*ability or power* to receive) was perfect. We were perfect in being, with the complete active potency to receive. But now, due to our originative self-impairment, we think instinctively of "receptivity" as a kind of passivity. Consequently, we think that God has to create all creatures as essentially active-passive, and not simply as essentially active-receptive.

In the process of doing philosophy and even doing theology, the cosmological notion of receptivity that is equivalent to passivity has been carried over to the ontological and the creational. Thereby a massive injustice is done to God's *infinity* of power, goodness, and love.

The idea that every created person is a unique *finite pure act of being* has to be abominable to minds with a cosmic fixation. Laboring with an understandably Aristotelian deprivation and undertow, they are unconsciously forced to think that God creates beings that are necessarily defective—beings supposedly not as pure as God is pure. They are cosmo-locked—mentally locked into a cosmic frame of being, keeping existence and being as practically synonymous terms.

Perhaps, at least some theologically attuned expositors are unwittingly confusing two "actions": the procession of infinite, *uncreated* Persons within the Godhead *and* the bringing of creatures to be. An unconscious pantheistic assumption can be made, in which *infinite participation* in the Being of God—proper only to the divine Persons—is serving as the unconscious standard of *perfection* for a creature. But a creature's perfection can only be finite, and *never* infinite or somehow part of God—even in the glory of heaven forever.

In any event, faith and reason beg for insight into God gifting every created person with *the purely active potency to receive being*. This finite active potency would entail no passive potency at all. Created persons, immediately and fully exercising this purely active potency to receive, would *be* perfectly who they are in freedom and in truth.

But *fallen* free persons like us would have caused their own *passive* potency. By the first exercise of their perfect freedom to receive, they partly failed to receive being fully. Multitudes of created persons willed *less than fully* to receive who they were being gifted to be.

Other created human persons, by their first act, might have willed *not to receive at all* their being. (They refused to "do God's will"). Thereby they would have sealed themselves off completely from the grace of God and immediately suffered everlasting ruin.

Those created humans who said *fully yes* to originative creation would have confirmed themselves as true to God—as finite, unique, *pure acts* of *be*-ing—immediately, ecstatically, and forever.

We could have been among them. Obviously, we are not.

Chapter 6

Receptivity and the Will of God

In this life, we always find active and passive receptivity together. So, it is not surprising that we can be quite confused about their difference.

We experience* no active receptivity that is *purely* active and not at all passive. Every agent or doer—from the activity of the tiniest microbe to the intuitions and love of a saint—is attempting to actuate or fulfill passive potencies. Each agent acts with potency or receptivity that is passive, as well as active.

A peach tree, for instance, has the active potency to "do peaches"—not apples or pears. But it also is "done *to*"— affected by the very peaches that it activates. Not to mention "being-done-to" by sunshine, rain, and so much else that serve to modify and determine the tree. All cosmic substances* have both active and passive potency.

The confusion between receptivity and passivity has clouded even the greatest philosophical-theological reflections on creation and redemption. The usual thinking rightly deems any being with passive potency to exist in an essentially incomplete or imperfect way. But it also holds that all of God's finest creatures are basically passive in *be*-ing—even the good angels.

Passivity, however, means being able "to be done to" or "determined by" another, as it were, from the outside. (Or to be determined by oneself as whole to part.) Passivity is the opposite of active potency: the ability to do, to act, to determine—to do the determining or specifying.

But our first glimpses of these kinds of potency find them ensconced in the world of passive matter and motion. Active potency is first known as it is in the crashed and recovering world, not in the ontological world from which it really originates.

A more refined meaning of potency would reveal *also* a "third kind" of receptivity, that is, an ability *to do-with*: to be-*with* and to act-*with* God and all others. This meaning would be *consonant with* the interpersonal act of *God being infinitely receptive*, that is, doing-*with* and being-*with* created persons wherever possible.

Better insight would reveal that God could only cause originatively—out of nothing—perfect created persons with perfect finite *capacity* to respond freely. The idea of originative creation as a personal act of the Creator causing immediately and *directly* any subpersonal beings would be seen for what it is: *absurd*. It would mean that at least some of the immediate results of sheer creation *out of nothing* would be intrinsically imperfect. God's prime effects would be less than perfect: an outcome "more impossible" than a square circle.

In creating us *ex nihilo*, God must have said, "Be" and "Be *with* Us." Every *affirming* creature must have responded immediately in full gratitude: "I *am with* you." Every rejecting creature must have said, "I *am against* you." Some, like us, must have said, "I *hesitate to be* with you." We failed to *be-with* fully, or to *do* our *being-with* fully.

It is extremely important to realize that, in this supreme activity of beginning to *be* and in receiving our being, *no temptation* could have been involved. There was nothing "outside," from which temptation could arise. We could not be "done to" in any way. We were not being tempted.

But we—and all persons being created—were *invited to be-with from within* the depths of our gifted beings. The invitation to being and to being-*with* might be said to include the issue of whether we would be willing to be simply finite, as gifted, in the infinite presence of the Persons of God.

Our pristine will was *perfectly free* to affirm fully the goodness of being, yet *able* to demur. In its fresh, God-gifted being, our *will* could not be *tempted*. It was *fully active*, but did not necessarily *fully act*.

The first free response to being-at-all—an act of non-durational, totally free self-determination—must have been an *untempted* response. No pulls or tugs or pushes. The response was immediate, free, and totally ours from within. (In order to realize that sin does not necessarily entail temptation, we might only have to ask the question, even under the perennial interpretation, "Who *tempted* Lucifer to sin?") And, of course, there was no question of space or time being involved in an *originative* creation of *be-ing*. Space and time are measures in and of *becoming*, not of *being*.

Each created person is *fully receptive*—actively, not passively—*as gifted by God* and receives *fully or not so fully* the gift of being by *doing* that being itself. The received being receives self *well or poorly*, freely and entirely from within—with a freedom much deeper than any "choice." Choices emerge in the derivative and relative freedom of *maybe*-sayers, whose *maybe* to *being* causes the *existence* of alternatives.

God's Best Needs No Test

Every being as created *directly* by God is perfect. God does not test "God products." It would be absurd to "test" the freedom of a person as created "*ex nihilo*" by God. "Perfection by God" is strictly untestable.

Pristinely created persons are perfectly *able* to respond to God with a full *yes*. The issue is their *potential* response; it is not their actual response. Their potential response is perfect, and free of passivity.

Only persons who are imperfect are testable and susceptible to an attempt to find how strong or weak they are. Temptation presupposes an already wounded nature.

That is what happened to Adam and Eve in the Garden of Eden. They were tempted. But they had already failed *the signature freedom of their being in the first, non-durational, untempted response—along with all of us—to the gift of being-at-all.* Only in their *actual* response to creation *ex nihilo* might they have caused flaws in *being* and made themselves imperfect.

Finite persons were *able* to make themselves imperfect because they were *finite* and not infinite. They *acted* imperfectly with their giftedly *perfect power* of *freedom*.

Some might think that, because Jesus was tempted in the desert, God was testing the Perfect One. But this was not temptation in the strict sense. It was temptation on the part of the tempter, but not on the part of the supposedly tempted one, since the divine Person *could* not sin. The Word of God is *infinitely free* not to sin.

For life among us in the world of sin and redemption, Christ assumed our *wounded* human nature. His incarnate human nature was susceptible to being afflicted and tormented, even slain, but could not be susceptible to *being* sinful. Jesus could not sin, and thereby could not have been tempted in the strict sense. Tormented, yes; tempted, no.

By *our* originative *act* of failing to be the perfect gift of freedom that we *are*, we set ourselves up for having to be conceived in space and time in the line of Adam. That *originative* sin was the *reason why* we were in the line of *original* sin at all—able to be "done to" or "done in" by others, most auspiciously by Adam and Eve, who had been tempted in Eden and let themselves be "done in" by Satan.

There is a good reason *why* we inherited the sin of Adam, and it is not simply because we were children of Adam. Rather, the opposite. We were children of Adam because of this reason: we primally, though partially, rejected the gift of being and the Giver at the initial moment of our *be*-ing.

Infinite Being was not *forced* to clunk us with the "original sin" of Adam. We made ourselves vulnerable to its infliction by our own incomparably more serious, *originative* sin—done along with Adam and at least billions of other human persons at the moment of being infinitely and super-intimately loved into being. Our having been generated in space and time is *part* of the redemptive process on which our recovery turns.[10]

---

[10] Much logical mischief has supported the idea that the human person is a "rational animal." But animality comes from the crash, for which we are responsible personally, not God. We are no more rational animals than an animal is a sentient plant. We are humans, not at all animals, despite the heavy likenesses at the superficial level of cosmogenic thought. Aristotle did his best in classifying

Nobody Is "Done to" by God

The creation of angels and of any other kind of person could not have been a "determination" from the outside, as *from* and *by* another. Creation *out of nothing* is not the same as causation—at least not the kind of causation with which we are so familiar in this material and fallen world of attempted recovery. As far as creation is concerned, God did not "do it *to* us." Before creation there was no "us" to be done *to*. (The "before" designates a priority of *being*, not of time and duration.)

God gifted us with *being*, without rendering us passive in the least. We received from infinite Being a finitely perfect being, totally active in potency, able to create a perfect response to God's gift, *by that gift itself*. We were thoroughly self-determining beings.

God determined *that* we would be and the *kind* of person (or self-determining being) we would be—angel or human—and *who* each of us would be, as well. But *that* kind of determination is quite different from the causal determinations we see in physical nature and in all of our self-activities of cosmic conditioning. *That* kind of determination is also different from anything represented

humans from a kind of cosmological perspective. Later philosophers, including Christians, have failed to clarify the *genus* and specific difference involved.

Ontologically speaking, humans are in the *genus* of person, along with the angels and God. Humans should be viewed—if the term *genus* is to be used—as rational *persons*, not rational animals. Intuitively rational. We are distinct in being intuitively rational, not purely intuitive. God-like, but not gods; animal-like, but not animals. Neither angels nor God are *rational* persons, that is, capable of reasoning.

The decimating cultural effects of the *rational animal* definition are decisively treated by Mary R. Joyce in her book, *The Future of Adam and Eve: Power for Wisdom about Love* (St. Cloud, MN: LifeCom, 2008).

in *Genesis* 1, where there is nothing but the slightest possible symbolic reference to the angels.[11]

Before we were "in being," so to say, we were *not* determin*able*. There is no passive potency in non-being. Once we were gifted, as it were "from within," with a determinate self, that self was *receivable* by that self itself—a self to be received well or not well. The receiving was *done*—however perfectly or poorly—*entirely by* the created self, and not by God *for* the self.

God creates self-creative beings. There is nothing *passive* about God's infinite act of creating, *nor* about the created person's *finite power to act* in response to this gift. Only a less-than-perfect, free response by the creature could have constituted any *passive* potency in and of the created being itself.

By our own free first (untempted) exercise of our act of *be*-ing we "did ourselves in." We botched our response to the invitation to be simply *this* uniquely finite being. We *passivized ourselves* by an abuse of our freedom, leaving ourselves "wide open" to *reactive* interaction with other passivized beings.

So, contrary to our most ardent wishes, everyone in the present world of space and time is responsible for the *origin* of his or her own suffering...unless that person is somehow a co-redeemer with Christ.

---

[11] St. Augustine saw the creation of angels as symbolized in the earliest reference of *Genesis* to the creation of light. Not an invalid surmisal.

But darkness preceding light would seem to indicate that the rebellious angels were created first. Why would bad angels precede good angels if all were created good?

In any event, the creation accounts in *Genesis* should be taken as referring, principally and overwhelmingly, to the creation of the cosmic world, with "the heavens" referring to the stars and planets in their cosmic setting.

Here we are: all "spaced out" and "doing time." We are now fully responsible as individuals for doing our best to learn *why* we are responsible and to learn *how* to do well the consequent suffering. For such purposes, the Redeemer brought us his body, the Church.[12]

---

[12] If we can believe that the man Jesus Christ was God the Word, we can entertain the possibility of a perfect creation and an immediate, originative sin. We are aided by contemplating the awesome suffering of Christ—physically, emotionally, mentally, and spiritually—for each of us, alone and together.

Chapter 7

A Profound Challenge of Being

Perennial theological reflection on the meaning of Revelation has yielded much light. But we have hardly attained an adequate understanding of the doctrines within Revelation and what the *infinity* of divine Being really means.

The question is not about coming to a *comprehensive* understanding. We ardently desire, rather, some kind of basic explanation that is adequate to our time and conditions of reflective consciousness. No one ever has completely comprehensive knowledge of anything, much less God. We do not know all there is to know about a blade of grass. Chlorophyll production is but a *part* of the being and existence of grass.

Light on the *infinity* of God has been offered at times. Nonetheless, theologians and philosophers often seem satisfied with calling God the all-perfect, all-powerful, all-good Being, and the like. But God is not simply a perfect being. Such an idea is really a dumbing down of God. God is the *infinite* perfection.

Our minds tend to be satisfied with the notion of *perfection* as strictly applicable *only* to God. We then infer, consciously or unconsciously, that we are imperfect even in our originative creation. It becomes commonplace to assume that to be a creature is to be imperfect. We do not necessarily say it that way, but rather imply that it is so.

The confusion involves identifying infinity as perfection, rather than as the supreme *kind* of perfection. If infinity is identified as perfection, then "finity" or finitude—proper only to creatures—is thought to be necessarily and intrinsically imperfect.

The mentality that "only God is perfect" can serve well to hide our originative condition: being a perfect person. We should realize that each of us *persons* were once perfect, as created by God. But we do not *want* to know that. So, the claim is repressed. We do not *let* ourselves be conscious of its truth.

We are called to know, however, that finitude is intrinsically *perfect*, precisely as a whole gift of God, who is *infinitely good and infinitely powerful.* God *could not* create an imperfect being or imperfect freedom, even as God could not create a square circle, a sinful soul, or an infinite creature.

Consider the ideas of "an originatively imperfect creature" and "an infinite creature." Both ideas are absurd. We see how an "infinite creature" is impossible, but we assume that "mere creatures" can actually be or must be originatively imperfect. That assumption reveals the ultimate origin of our problems of low "self-esteem."

We are so inclined to hide from ourselves the depths of our responsibility that we *will not* admit that God gifted us with a perfect finite being, with the perfect active potency to respond fully. Our free, personal, incomplete response to our being has virtually disabled us from affirming completely the goodness of all being and of the *infinite* goodness of God.

We originatively faltered and repressed our being-full (ontological) responsibility. Consequently, we are now suffering from the dumbing down of *being*. In the history of our struggle to understand ourselves, this impairment in self-consciousness remains, despite advances such as the Thomistic insight into the *meaning* of being.

Only with tremendous effort and development did we come to realize with Thomas Aquinas the unique meaning of being and its implications for theistic faith. Plato and Aristotle had evidenced remarkable meaning for being. Beyond them, Thomas affirmed the ontological continuity between God as Pure Act of Being and creatures as participated acts of *being*.

Yet, despite his historic breakthrough in the meaning of being and in conceiving the infinity of God, Aquinas failed to see the implication for creation *ex nihilo*. Granted that God freely wills to create, *the infinite power of God means it is possible, and the infinite goodness of God means it is necessary*, for God to create *out of nothing* only perfect finite beings.

The finitude and freedom of every one of these created persons are perfect, flawless, complete. In the gifting of being, God does God's *infinite* "part" by gifting *perfectly*; and the created persons are called to do their *finite* part by receiving themselves perfectly.

But we obviously wavered and failed. Our defective finite response—in contrast to that of multitudes of angelic persons, at least—is the cause of passive potencies of every kind. In consort with Aristotle, who studied the universe with hardly a sense of original sin, Aquinas seemed to assume that only God was pure act. Somehow, he then inferred that *created beings* were *not* pure acts. He thus attributed passive potency even to the angelic creatures whose originative responses to God were, in effect, immediately and completely *yes*.

Instead, being *as being*—*not* being as ex-isting—could have been seen as perfect, whether uncreated or created. Being as gifted—creatures *ex nihilo*—could have been recognized as necessarily *perfect* (not infinite) in freedom, goodness, power, and so forth. The originative creating act of God could have been understood as *gifting* only pure active potency and pure acts of finite being, who are persons only. No animals, plants, and inanimate entities could have been created *directly* by *God alone*, since the essences of these creatures are intrinsically imperfect.

Persons Are Perfect in the Immaculate Creation

We know of three kinds of persons: divine, angelic, and human. The essence of a divine person is to be and to be infinite. The essence of an angelic person is to be and to be *simply* finite. The essence of a human person is to be and to be *complexly* finite.

Each finite person is a unique act of be-ing. But, besides the unlimited uniqueness of God, there are two kinds of limited uniqueness: simple, and complex.

God is both infinite simplicity of being and infinite richness of relationships. Angelic beings are like God in the richness of their relationships, but especially in their simplicity. Human persons are like God in their simplicity, but especially in the richness of their relationships.

Angels have no capacity for receiving their essence, but simply for receiving their act of being. Their essence as receptivity for their being is simple. So, such persons could only say immediately *either* fully *yes* or fully *no* to

God in creation. It was that simple and decisive forever. Their commitment to, or rejection of, God, self, and others was simple and total.

Unlike the simplicity of the angels, human receptivity is complex. Human persons are doubly receptive. They are receptive not only of their act of being, but also of the essential form* itself. This capacity to receive the form of the essence is an *active* potency, and not at all a passive one. This receptivity is really *active matter* that can become passive-reactive matter if the form is only *partially* received. Passivity originates from the *no* in the *maybe*. But the reaction against passivity originates in the *yes*.

Originatively, in the immaculate creation, matter *is* the purely active potency for receiving the human "form." And the essential (substantial) form is the purely active potency to give self to self and others. Form is *givity* (purely active) and matter is receptivity (purely *active*).

But, in our case, *matter* had partially collapsed into passive potency, and *form* into ontological acquisitiveness. Both principles became principles within the redemptive creation. The human *maybe*, because of the *no* within it, reduces the *active* potency within the essence—both the form and the matter—to the condition of being a passive-reactive potency for redemptive recovery.

Because of the active potency within the immaculately created human essence, the human person—not the angelic person—was able to say *yes, no*, or *maybe*. Angels were "unable to hesitate" about being finite. There was nothing about their unique essences by which they could hesitate as to what *intensity* of their *essence* they would be *willing* to be.

In its gifted state, human receptivity was active and perfect, pure receptivity—*matter*, but with *no* passivity whatsoever. Human persons who exercised this pure receptivity of essence by saying fully *yes* united themselves directly with God, as did multitudes of angelic persons. But those who said *maybe* thereby failed to *receive fully* both their being and their own God-gifted essence, *from right within the essence itself.* They created a passivity of essence—passive receptivity or passive *matter*.

Matter as pure receptivity turned passive and apt for a body. Such matter, bodily matter—the kind we know so well now—is *inherently functional* and far from the celebrational matter with which we were gifted originatively.

Human persons, then, are originatively *both* like angels *and* different from angels. Like angels, they could receive their *being* directly and fully; but unlike angels they also had receptivity in their essence. So, they could say fully *yes*, fully *no*, or *maybe*, that is, with hesitation as to what degree they were receiving their being. They were more complex than angels. They could, so to speak, "control" their own essence.

Such was a less perfect *kind* of being than that of the angels. But this human kind of person was perfect, nonetheless.[13] The partial failure of multitudes—failure to

---

[13] Lack of clarity respecting the likeness and difference between angels and humans is shown in the recent translations of *Psalms* 8:6 about God creating humankind "a little less than the angels." Some of the recent English editions have rendered the text with expressions such as "a little less than God," or "a little less than gods." Important ontological work is needed to challenge the suggestion that any created person is to be "compared" to God, and to support the traditional understanding of the relationship between created persons: angelic and human. We are supremely related to God, but are in nowise comparable. The

receive both their own act of being and their own essence fully—caused an implosion of their *being* upon itself. They fractured their own actuality as received persons. Due to the *no* in their hesitation about fully receiving their essence, their matter (receptivity) collapsed. But due to the *yes*, their matter (contaminated receptivity) reacted in the form of chaotic energy.

God's response to the reactive *yes* was redemptive Love. Divine love transformed the chaotic energy into creative energy for the redemptive recovery of hesitating persons.

The result became a great explosion of energy, through which came forth the development of the spatiotemporal cosmos. This energy is the "capacity to do work," namely, *some* of the basic work of God's *redemptive* creation within the *immaculate* creation. So much of the "spiritual work" is our life's unseen drama.

In their essence, human persons had the ability to respond by saying simply *yes* or simply *no*. But they could also respond somewhere between *yes* and *no*. They could cause a stall, if they willed to do so. This aspect of their essence is their matter, the originative principle of receptivity. Although demeaned and passivized, this somewhat receptive matter made them redeemable. Such is the goodness of our matter; it is not fully self-rejected. Nonetheless, originative matter had fallen from active receptivity into "active passivity."[14]

---

interpretations around the use of the words, *elohim* and *angelos*, need a sound ontological referee.

[14] In scholastic terminology, prime matter is considered to be sheerly passive potency. While there is a kind of "logical truth" about this notion of prime matter being complete passivity, the ontological reality is surmised by Aristotle and others who think of prime matter as an appetite for any and all forms. This dynamic concept is further enhanced by Thomas Aquinas who regarded prime matter as "similitudo formae," a "likeness of form."

Cosmic creaturehood—including all imperfections found in the being and behavior of subpersonal cosmic creatures—should be acknowledged as being the result of an emanation from the originative *failure* of *completely* flawless created (human) persons to receive their own beings *completely*. All cosmic energy could be recognized as a redemptive effluent from the crash of the being of multitudes of human persons. And in our thinking, then, we would not saddle God with being the *sole* cause of the cosmos *as we now know it*.

Aquinas could not sufficiently transcend the Aristotelian-Platonic framework that had been so helpful to the development of his philosophy and theology. So, we have continued to conflate *being* and *becoming*. And we have effectively treated the redeeming activity of God as a kind of mega-codependency. We think that in creating us, as well as in redeeming us, God keeps us ever more dependent.

Dependency on God for becoming and for salvation is necessary and even crucial. We are normally far from sufficiently dependent on God in everyday life and in the depths of our soul.

But we seem unaware that it is our *willed* (independent) dependence on God that will make it possible for God to free us from sin, so that we can be forever independent-*with* God, self, and others. We are called to live our identity—on the cross of paradox—as beings of *both* dependence *and* independence.

Independence-*with*

We need a paradigm shift in theology and philosophy. Our primary relationship with God, quite different from our redemptive relationship, is not one of dependence, but of independence. We are related to God in creation *ex nihilo* by an independence-*with* God, not an independence-from or –of God.

We seem to be completely unaware of the originative gift of being independent-*with* God. We are conditioned to think that *to be*, as such, is not necessarily to be perfect. We are taught that only God is perfect. God, it is assumed, directly creates birds, and trees, and the ocean breeze, without any "interference" from created persons.

Nevertheless, these and other assumptions continue to keep us from realizing our radical personal responsibility for being the kind of human being we are—and for existing as we are. We continue the blame chain right back to God as we *unconsciously*, if not consciously, blame God for the plight of humans *existing* in the Garden of Eden with all of *its* passive potency. And we blame God for being unable to prevent our inheriting of the sin of Adam in that Garden.

Who seems aware of—or ready to question—this predicament of Adam and Eve living in a world of temptation? And who asks *why* temptation occurred in the first place—in Eden or anywhere else? We are apparently oblivious of the underlying base of Adam's world.

That base is to be found in an infinitely-good and infinitely-powerful God who originatively gifts perfectly created persons with their *being*—the *immaculate creation*.[15] We are dumbing down *being* because the notion of God as *really infinite* is *really* missing.

---

[15] Incidentally, the very word "perfect" etymologically signifies completion of a process of making (*per facere*). But perennial usage seems to have purged it of any necessary denotation of "imperfection."

Evolution Is *Not* the Originative Creation

The conduct of the creationist-evolutionist controversy is a major manifestation of the missing infinity of God. And it represents well our repression of the perfection of originative creation. Many theistic thinkers are identifying the process of evolution with God's original creation.

Under the influence of several 20^(th) century thinkers, especially Teilhard de Chardin, many theologians have been gravitating toward an evolutionist interpretation of creation *ex nihilo*. The missing infinity of God should be blatantly evident in this kind of theology.

The error is not the attribution of evolution's causality to God's activity. The great mistake is the failure to recognize evolution as, at best, *part* of God's *redemptive* (*ex aliquo*) *creation* of persons—and *not at all a part* of creation *out of nothing*. It is possible that, by means of a kind of evolution, persons could recover partly from their originative faltering response to being created and to the crash of their being at the moment of *originative* (*ex nihilo*) creation.

Creationists, of course, react to theistic evolutionism. But their position is hardly an improvement. Creationism shares with theistic evolutionism the false assumption that creation *out of nothing* can be a *process*. For creationists, of course, the process of creation is relatively quick. But this "week-long" series of creation activities on God's part does not seem to strike them as grossly incongruous with an infinite Being acting infinitely and originatively.

Neither side in the ensuing controversy recognizes the true nature of creation as a gift of *personal being*—and *not* a making or a process of *any* kind. The idea that God *originatively* created us through evolution, creationism, or any other "process" of creation shows how we absurdly disregard the unlimited magnificence of the Infinite Being.

There is no process *in or of God*. Nor does process exist by the activity of God alone. Process is the *activity of imperfect creatures*—whether they are regenerating or degenerating—responding positively or negatively to God's ever-present, infinite love.

In an attempt to show God's care and empathy, many contemporary theologians have slipped into becoming process philosophers. They continue to assume an intrinsic relationship of dependency or even interdependency between God and creatures. But the attempt at "process thinking" about God is not dynamic; it is incomparably passive, representing "dynamically" our denial of the perfect creation and of our originative sin.

We will not admit to ourselves a personal, pristine sin committed at the non-durational moment in which our being was created whole and entire out of nothing. So, even while sometimes using the *term* infinite, we unconsciously reach for one or more notions of a "less than real infinity" and project them unwittingly onto God. Or we incorporate God into our own manner of defective finite being.

Religious thinkers have talked commonly about creation as a production. (The classic definition is *productio rei ex nihilo sui et subjecti*.) They even refer to the "production" or infusion of the human soul as occurring at the moment of conception.*[16] But we never hear even a speculation

---

[16] We come to the moment of conception with lots of baggage. It is not the beginning of our being, but of our becoming—be-ing trying to come back to itself through eventual growing awareness, repentance, and thanksgiving. Conception happens *to* us, who have originatively sinned. It does not "start" us absolutely, but starts us in this world of redemptivity. We are *conceived* in sin, as well as "die the death," because we already are sinners. God does not create any person "in sin."

about God creating us in our whole being of personhood, in *perfect* finitude. Another classic definition of creation, as an *emanation—emanatio totius esse*—has problems, too.

Actually, there is a profound reason why we rarely, if ever, find a theologian or philosopher talking about creation as an *interpersonal* act. It would require us to admit responsibility for any and all evil that reaches us. Not that we, as spatiotemporal agents, are directly causing much of the evil that afflicts us now, but that we caused ourselves *originatively* to be *susceptible* to evil-at-all and to *being here* as *cosmic* creatures in the first place.

At any rate, I am claiming that, without any process at all, we were created as perfect persons with perfect freedom to respond immediately to the gift of being and of being-*with* God. If we have any doubt, we might consider seriously the following truth: We are now shattered and scattered as persons and as prospects for fulfillment of our being.

God *could not* have created—*pristinely, out of nothing—* this "chaos." God could have created *directly only* the free agents who created the primeval chaos. God's relation to the disorder would include letting it serve to foster the *repentance* of the persons who caused it.

God's infinite love and infinite power engendered redemption. This infinite love has been working with the whole of the originatively fallen humanity, ultimately empowering the redemptive energy that gradually formed itself into a *cosmos*. In the cosmic part of the recovery of repentant human personhood, there might indeed be involved a process—whether evolutionary, creationist, or partly both.[17]

In any case, for understanding the cosmic part of redemptive creation, we are required to engage in paradoxical thinking, including a *logic* of paradox. But confidently knowing that we are *both* independent-*with* God originatively *and* completely *dependent* on God for recovery is lacking in both the creationist and the evolutionist sides of the debate. Many labor contentedly *without awareness* of the profound challenge of beingful (ontological) understanding. Thus, the *flat being society* continues to prevail.

---

[17] The modern and contemporary debates between theistic evolutionists and creationists are an interesting overlay on the deeper questions of creation *ex nihilo* vs. creation *ex aliquo*. Until we can see better from the ontological perspective of *the immaculate creation*, both sides will continue making unresolvable claims.

Chapter 8

The Intimate Act of Creation

Many contemporary theologians are championing some kind of theistic evolution as a way to describe creation. A persistent question in evolution theory concerns the missing link between animals and human persons. These theologians think they can bridge the gap by their theories.

But this attention to a gap is trumped by a much deeper issue: what is the missing link between God's infinite Being and the immediate results of God's act of creation? They continue to neglect this great "missing link" that is much closer to home.

How can reality go from God as infinitely good and infinitely powerful to the void as the beginning of creation? Or to dust as the beginning of human persons?

This breach of ontological proportions might be reasonably depicted as created by the *first* exercise of our finite freedom, at the moment of originative creation.[18]

---

[18] Intellectual history suffers from many attempts at producing a type of explanation that amounts to a *deus ex machina*. The perennial way of explaining our beginning in earthly life with the sin of Adam is a major case in point. God is actually, if implicitly, blamed for allowing Adam to clunk us with a defective human nature as the result of the original sin. If we were really innocent of this disaster of original sin, by allowing it to happen God would not be God. Instead of facing our own responsibility for *be*-ing the way we are, we blame Adam and Eve explicitly and God implicitly, while saying that evil is a "mystery." (Next page.)

Of course, we would find it difficult—if we ever tried to do so—to describe even generally God's *act* of creation itself: an act at the non-durational, absolute moment of our being's beginning. But we can reasonably acknowledge that this interpersonal moment is real. We can also infer that now, as we come lamely into self-awareness here in the cosmos, we are living out the results of our pristine, *interpersonal* response to God's unconditional, *infinitely intimate* love.

God's *real infinity* is a principle that is usually missing in our reflections. Therefore, we do not see that God is "unable" to create—out of *nothing*—anything other than perfect persons with the perfect freedom to respond to their originative creation. Even to think that God could *possibly* create *directly* an imperfect being—even a slightly imperfect world—is to denigrate the *infinite* source of *interpersonal* intimacy.

God's act of creating us is an infinitely intimate act—not a temporal one, nor any kind of durational one. Time and space and all passive matter and motion, have their origins in something else: our pristine, but faulty *reception* of this infinite act of intimacy.

Time is not in the act of God who, with infinite freedom, graces finite freedom to be. Our *maybe* to being and to God caused time to "have to be" and to exist: a deformed, but hopeful, way of relating to eternity.

Of course, it is a mystery. And so is gravity, electricity, chlorophyll production, and every other natural and supernatural reality. Our intransigence is more than remarkable. This propensity to dodge originative sin is carried out in the creationism and evolutionism debates by our attempts to produce a "god of the gaps" theodicy. We will think almost anything rather than face the truth of our *personal* response to the *perfect creation*. Perhaps we need instead a "self of the gaps" theology.

We were *not* created as eternal beings. The One Eternal being is without either beginning or ending. We were created *by* eternity, for union *with* eternity. We had a beginning *in* eternity—not an "eternal beginning." And in that beginning we "prompted" the ex-istence of space and time.

God cannot create passive potency *ex nihilo.* To think so is to confuse infinity with arbitrarity.

We must have been created directly as pure acts of *potential* intimacy with God, as purely active finite potencies. We could not have been created directly as pure acts of *actual* intimacy, because intimacy comes only between beings who are *mutually* free to *let themselves be* intimate. Freedom is a necessary condition for genuine intimacy.

Our union with God forever can only come by virtue of *both* God's love *and* our *willing reception* of all the love, goodness, and power, of which our being is capable. There is no such thing as a divine *imposition* of intimacy and glory.

So, we are now obviously in a condition of *spiritual repression*—far more critical than any emotional or psychic repression. We ourselves must be repressing the moment of absolute creation that we once knew clearly and yet failed to receive fully. At that moment, our activity of *protoconsciousness* was a super-knowledge and super-freedom immensely purer than anything we know now by our gradually *awakening* kind of consciousness.

There is no other alternative for honesty in thought about an infinitely good agent loving us perfectly into being. Imperfection of being or activity can come only from created persons whose faltering freedom of will caused it—either by rejecting totally (angelic, human) or by hesitating (human). The only other alternative is that God is not who God is: the Being who is *infinite* in goodness, power, love, justice, and mercy.

Tragically, as originatively failing persons, we cannot— or will not—face the prospect that we freely, though partly, denied the being we received. We will not acknowledge that we thereby missed—then and perhaps forever—the everlasting intimacy with God, offered by creation *ex nihilo*.

Development within a creationistic or evolutionistic framework might be considered to be *part* of what is happening to us now. But such recuperatively processive activity is radically different from the inexorably perfect origin of our whole being and of our immediately personal response. Creation *ex aliquo* (out of *something*), such as would be creationism or evolution, is not at all the same as creation *ex nihilo* (out of *nothing*).[19]

In any event, one kind of development is certainly true. Human *thought* must "evolve." We must somehow be able to make a leap forward in our thinking to higher, more

---

[19] This new ontological aspect concerning creation and sin requires some new meaning for the issues of nature and grace. The grace of creation is the primary grace, the infinite offer of intimacy with God forever that could have been ours, but was partly refused. God's creation of our becoming (our being coming back from that self-distortion), delineated in *Genesis*, requires our wounded nature to receive the grace of redemption and salvation: grace (the supernatural, infinite life) "adds" to nature necessary healing for this purpose.

But in the originative creation (*ex nihilo*) there was the complete opportunity for unwounded, pristine nature to unite with supernatural, infinite nature immediately. All was both grace and nature: God's and ours. But we did not fully unite. We did not *grace* God with our whole beng. *With* and *in* Adam, we sinned. Thus, Adam's subsequent "original sin" could be considered as a "happy fault" and "necessary" only figuratively and only because we have repressed our personal participation in our own originative sin with Adam. There was really nothing "happy" about it.

In the new view, there is nothing that the infinite merits of Christ could add to the originatively *infinitely intimate* act of God in gifting us with a perfect personal being immediately *out of nothing*. Infinite love cannot be "added to." The grace of redemptive creation is a gift within the grace of originative creation.

perfect levels. Perhaps our ruminating about creation will have to advance so that we can realize the missing infinity of God and recognize how vacuous is the assignment of creationism or evolution as God's "mechanism" for creating us out of nothing.

Creationism and evolution are ever *ex aliquo* (out of *something*); they could never be *ex nihilo*. The process of development—however long or short—necessarily entails imperfection. Presumably whatever is more developed emerges from what is less developed. But the act of creation *ex nihilo* is not a process at all; it is an act of an infinite Being, gifting *being* to other persons who are thereby whole and free. It is completely an *inter*personal offer of everlasting intimacy: an immaculate creation.

Only Person-Beings Are Complete Beings

Another problem with both evolutionary creation and creationism is that these theories do not adequately acknowledge the difference between person-beings and thing-beings. A virtually equivalent ontological status is wrongly, if unconsciously, given to both persons and non-persons, as far as sheer creation is concerned.

So, we call trees *beings*, just as we call people *beings*. We seem to think that, after all, both kinds of being really *are*. And it is so. Both are real.

This use of the term *being*, as equivalently personal and non-personal, has a long history in Western philosophy. But such is merely cosmological consciousness, and it fails to respect the meaning of *being* in various ways.

Persons are complete beings. Animals, plants, and all other subpersonal beings are not. And the analyses we give to them in terms such as potency and act, matter and form—found in cosmology, for instance—*ought not then be applied directly* to persons *as person-beings*.[20]

These analytic terms are typically used in the context of physical nature with its degrees of passivity. They do not apply directly to personal finite beings, who are originatively pure acts: beings of purely active potency. In fact, such beings—*perfect* created persons, now imperfect and struggling, in space and time, to regain freedom—are not even recognized. Even in traditional metaphysics, pure acts of finite be-ing are thought to be impossible, contradictory.[21]

To the contrary, if infinite Being wills to create any beings at all, those beings are going to be *persons*, who are necessarily purely actual, free, and self-determining. They are beings that are created from a beginning without any qualification. These full-beings are *perfectly able to receive both themselves (the gifts) and the Giver*, in different ways. They do so by the powers of *knowing and loving*, in dimensions quite other than the logical and psychological. Such self-determining beings include all persons, angelic and human. They are created to be immediately (and freely) intimate with God and one another.

In contrast, subpersonal beings are part-beings. They only come to be through God's loving redemptive activity and as the result of some flaw, caused by the failure of many created, full-beings. Part-beings (subpersonal beings) exist without the critical powers of receptivity:

---

[20] The term cosmology is used loosely to designate what is known traditionally as the philosophy of nature or "general science of nature."

[21] This idea of finite pure acts of *be*-ing (*esse*) is an impossible supposition for minds that are philosophical captives of passive matter and motion, and whose metaphysics contains a latent pantheism concerning the meaning of Being. The cosmologic lock holds sway with many.

knowing and loving. They cannot truly *receive* their own being, much less the being of God. Nor can they truly *give* themselves *as selves* in being.

Indeed, at some point, the ancient Aristotelian principle must be applied that says *the order of knowing is the reverse of the order of being.* What we first come to know consciously about reality in this world is last in being or in the way things *are.* As a result, we can begin to acknowledge that the beings we know first and best—consciously—are various kinds of subpersonal ones. These beings (existents) are consequences of the *need* for redemption of persons in the cosmos.

Persons are the kind of beings that we consciously know later and with great difficulty. We self-knowing beings first come to know the physical dimensions of our nature more readily than our own spiritual depths. A human infant knows his or her toes, without, at first, even knowing consciously whose they are or what a toe is.

Analogously further, the order of being is not only the reverse of the order of knowing, but *also* the reverse of the order of becoming. Personal beings do not come—as persons—*from* subpersonal beings. Rather, subpersonal beings come by way of defectively responding persons, whose originative activity created in themselves a "fractuality" (fractured actuality). Out of the resultant cosmic *energy* of this ontological "big bang"—the "friction" between the *yes* and *no* of our originative response to being-at-all—the whole world of subpersonals was fashioned by divine activity: from the atomic and molecular to plants and animals.

In the process that is involved in the creation of becoming (being coming back), no subpersonal being becomes what it *is not*: a person-being. Nor can a person-being become what it *is not*: a subpersonal being. One being cannot *become* any other kind of being and still *be* itself. One being can only become more and more or less and less its own self or kind of self—more and more or less and less what it already *is*. Becoming is based in being.

Because we do not distinguish adequately between the creation of becoming and its base in the creation of being, the understanding of actual and potential being is readily confused at the highest levels. Sometimes theologians and philosophers will even speak of God as the "fully actualized Being," instead of saying *infinitely actual* Being. But there is nothing about God "to be actualized." Only a being with *passive* potency can be actual*ized*. God *is* actual. God is *not* fully actual, as though God could be only partly actual, but happens to be fully so. God is *infinitely actual* or *infinite actuality*.

Misconceiving God leads to intellectual mischief when conceiving creatures. For instance, limited being has come to be identified perennially as imperfect being. If God is thought to be Unlimited Being and Perfect Being, then there is a heavy tendency to assume that created persons are limited being *and imperfect* being.

Only the first pairing of the contrasts, however, is essentially true. God is unlimited and created persons are limited. But both God and created persons are perfect being: God as perfect Giver and created persons as perfect gifts.

It cannot be an imperfection to be finite rather than infinite. *As gifted by God,* persons must be both finite and perfect. Only *as received by themselves immediately-and-*

badly can they be imperfect or defective, suffering an inconceivable loss of intimacy with God.[22]

---

[22] There may be many or few *human* persons who received themselves immediately and fully, thereby confirming themselves forever in love and perfect finite harmony with God. They were therefore *not subject* to the "sin of Adam" or of any other sin.

Chapter 9

Our Independently Personal Freedom

We sometimes talk as though we think we "*ought* to be God." For instance, people who deliberately think that a created person is *imperfect because finite* (limited) would seem to imply that if this creature were perfect he or she would be infinite, namely, a divine Person.

This notion about being infinite might be quite unconscious, but real. Some might be hiding from themselves the thought: "How dare I lack infinity!" Alternatively, "How dare God give me an imperfect finite being. I want to be a divine Person." Whether the articulators actually intend the meaning or are merely going along with "an unconscious protocol" is an important question.

For theorists to make the error of identifying finitude (being limited) with imperfection may be to exhibit one symptom of our unconscious pride in being. We want to be our own God, even as Adam and Eve did.

It seems likewise *incredible* that we could have contracted this inherent pride *simply* through the sin of a first couple. Would we not have, as well, the *vulnerability* for this sin? Are we not responsible *on our own* for being *able* to be so *involved* in the "sin of Adam"? Why were we *susceptible at all* to the sin of human persons who are *other than* ourselves? Is God really not able to create us independent with respect to sinful parents, giving us sinless parents or no parents at all? Adam and Eve, for instance, had no parents.

The only ground for understanding why we "took the hit" is our "hit-ability": a condition that could only come ultimately *from us* and our initial acting with full freedom of being, as gifted by God. This originative freedom and activity on our part is *beingfully* (ontologically)—not temporally—"prior" to any socially sinful condition, including the inheritance of the sin of Adam and Eve.

Even if one thinks that it was the sin of Adam that initially and severely damaged our *common human* nature, one still needs to inquire about our *individual nature*— Joe's Joe*ness* and Jane's Jane*ness*. Are we, as individuals, the captives of our common human nature; or is common human nature the communal support of a multitude of *individual* personal natures?

Are we a bit like bees in a hive and like individuals of an animal species? Are we condemned or locked into being high-class functionaries of our clan, our nation, our planet, our humanhood? If so, there can really be no further development or the advance of freedom in the *human* consciousness. We are then ultimately only extensions of Adam's nature, and *not of our own*. We are merely pan-Adamic or pan*adam*istic.

Human free activity, however, is not merely generic activity. Only by unique persons taking variously free initiatives could there be development in the communal consciousness of persons conceived in space and time, matter and motion.

A human person is never subpersonal, no matter how much human behavior would so appear. To *be* a person, whether angelic or human, is to *be able*—naturally, if not always functionally in the case of earthly humans—to act independently of the actions of beings of the same or similar kind.

Our sluggish consciousness would constrain us into evaluating human behavior as partly animal and species-specific. Instead, we might begin to realize that all human actions are those of, and by, persons *as unique persons*—no matter how impeded by cosmic conditions they indeed may be. Even human actions of breathing, eating, and sleeping are full-being acts of a person, not of an animal—despite the heavy, overt, even obvious, yet ultimately superficial similarities.

Again, we need to apply the classic principle about our way of *conscious* knowing: our coming to know things is the reverse of the way those things *are*. We first come to know, consciously and emphatically, our plant-*like* and animal-*like* potentialities and operations—our physical growing, assimilating, breathing, sensing, and so forth. Only gradually and with considerably more difficulty, do we begin to know our deeper life of self-reflection and freedom, and its potential—including the ontological and spiritual origin of our strictly human sensory powers.

At a deeper level, moreover, we can say that we first come to know what it is to be *limpingly* human: having all kinds of needs, desires, aspirations, strengths, and weaknesses. Only later do we begin to know, and to take responsibility for, what it means to *do* and *be* the unique and everlasting human person that we are—and have been.

We transcend, while including, our membership in common humanity. The uniqueness of being *this* human, of being *this* person, cannot be taken away from us by our family, our clan, our tribe, and our fellowship in the human community. We are beings of both a common essence (human personhood) and a unique essence (*this* personhood).

By our unique ability for self-determination, we can act fully against our "species" and our family, or we can fulfill and surpass them brilliantly. Heaven and hell are not species-specific. We ultimately arrive there as unique human *individuals*: Jane in all her Janeness, Joe in all his Joeness.

Limits and the Meaning of *Genesis*

Many people assume that to have limits is to be defective and lacking perfection. Limits are deemed to be indications of weakness or inadequacy. But defect-limits are not the only kind of limits.

Instead, limits should be recognized, first of all, as boundaries of identity that are quite natural and essential to the being of created persons. There is nothing imperfect about the pristinely finite being. To be limited is quite proper to a created person and says nothing about there being any defect in that person. This being is simply *this* being and not any other. To be a created person is a limit, but not a defect.

Even God is "limited" to being uncreated and not to being, *as God*, created. God is "limited" to being unlimited. Actually, both God (including the Triune Persons) and every created person are *unique*. There is nothing "limiting" about being uniquely who one is.

In some sense, even God the Father is "limited" to being Father Person *and not* Word Person or Spirit Person. The "limitation of identity" applies even to the infinitely unique Persons of divinity.

If any person were created *ex nihilo* as *defectively* limited, God would not be the Creator. A created person would. That is the only way defect-limits could come to be "out of nothing"—by a supposition contrary to possibility.

In fact, the story of *Genesis*—received without a breakthrough in ontology—would seem to lead us into thinking of God not as a perfect Creator, but as a Super-craftsman, a defective creator—with Adam coming from "dust" and Eve from a "rib." But this story should be taken to pertain to God specifically as *Redeemer*, not as Creator of persons *ex nihilo*. God redeems by creating us *ex aliquo* (*out of something*)—out of the mess (the void or chaos) *we* at once made of the perfect gift of our being *ex nihilo*. This divine, redemptive activity culminates in the incarnate sacrifice of the Word of God in the "fullness of time."

Redemptive creation is God's activity of gradually restoring us—at the cost of our immense resistance that is almost totally unconscious—to the fullness of unique being that God gifted to us in the first place (*ex nihilo*). We are not only resisting God, but also denying our own perfect giftedness of being.

Rather than the story of a creation of *being*, *Genesis* is the story of a creation of be-*coming* (being coming back). The creation of angels is not explicitly involved. Full-beings (human persons who made themselves quite imperfect *ontologically*) are attempting to come back to their originative wholeness by their moral efforts. Among other ways, they struggle through interaction with the errant energies of subpersonal existence. Cosmic matter is constituted by the fragmentive human energy caused by the originative crash of human *freedom*.

Apparently, the whole of Scriptural Revelation deals only indirectly with the *interpersonal* activity of God *ex nihilo*, gifting perfect beings who are perfectly free to respond.[23] It seems to assume that originative creation was perfect.

The Originative Gift of Being Is Not Dependence on God for Salvation

We are *absolutely dependent* on God. But that critical dependency occurs because of our first *response* to creation and because of our present, wounded and sinful *exile*. Dependency is not the result of the gift of our be-ing. We *depend* on God to save us from total and everlasting ruin. Only God can save us. But we do *not depend* on God as a result of the perfect creation.

Our be-ing is an absolute *gift*, not a loan. And it is not a gift as gifts are given in the highly imperfect world of space and time. Such gifts are given out of circumstances, not "out of nothing."

Somehow we inveterately conflate the crucially *needed* creation of our *becoming*—proper to our redemption—with the originative creation of our *being*. We then readily overlook the paradox in our relationship with God: we are *both* dependent *and* not dependent with respect to God.

Spiritually, we tend readily to acknowledge our radical dependence arising from our sin. *That* is very good. But then, simultaneously, we attribute it *also* simply to our being *creatures*. We are blocked and harbor little awareness of the special, gifted relationship of *non-*

---

[23] There are a few possible exceptions in Scripture, such as 2 *Maccabees* 7:28. In this and other texts, the *ex nihilo* might be suggested, but the necessarily interpersonal character of the act seems merely implied.

dependence emanating from our being inter*personal* with God.

Failure to think paradoxically is the bane of all ontological and theological thinking. If we are going to make progress in understanding anything of traditional value, we must keep, front and center, our "both-and" mentality (the potential for appreciating paradox). Lack of paradox-power leads to unnecessary confusion.

The confusion comes from our present condition of being *cast out* and in dire need. We live and think within the workings of the whole *cosmic* universe of supreme interdependence. And from there we draw our most immediate meanings—even for deeper philosophical and theological truths.

Our implicit, but almost inevitable, model for relations between cause and effect, for instance, comes naturally from our situation in space and time. In this world of be-*coming*—of passive matter and motion—every effect is intrinsically dependent upon its agent cause or causes, and every agent cause is necessarily dependent—even if not intrinsically—upon its effect and the matter with which it works. The normal wind "depends" on the tree's branches, not the trunk or roots, to cause palpable motion of the tree. The painter depends on the qualities of the pigment and canvas while effecting a painting.

This essential dependency in space and time is an ontological reality. We not only *think* of it that way; it *is* that way. *As we exist* in this world *of passivities*, to be related *is* to be dependent.

When we first come to know the world of matter and motion—and as we are still knowing it now—we see that one thing depends on others to exist and to come to exist. And our traditional meaning for causality—derivable largely from "common sense"—is gleaned from this condition of universal dependency of effects on their causes in the whole world of redemptive activity— including the spiritual.

In this mega-recuperative framework, every effect is less than a sheer gift. Every effect is part of a whole *process* of nature striving to differentiate itself, more and more, toward further conditions of heightened being and becoming. Even the essentially spiritual world of purgatory involves causal dependencies.

But we can notice something else. Nothing in space and time *is*, in and of itself, simply *a sheer, unfunctional gift* of its Uncreated Creator. Everything is immensely functional and in need of others for functioning at all. In a *functional* world, gifts are *never pure* gifts. They are largely aids or resources for existence and activity. But, because of our deeply spiritual streaks of consciousness, flowing from our preconscious union with the realm of sheer being, we can recognize them as "gifts."

If we take into account this world merely as it exists now, God cannot be really regarded as the simple Gifter of being. God is inevitably taken to be the Great Ontological Functionary. The divine Being is "naturally," but falsely, thought to create only dependent beings, who are passive with respect to their own activity and are basically functionaries of God. Such creatures are notably *unlike* God, *both* in being finite *and* in being dependent and passive.

We are called to affirm the paradox—to carry the cross of meaning. This world is basically good and beautiful. It is not basically evil and ugly. But it is also chaotic: a self-differentiating, organized confusion underpinned by entropy. Persons here are vulnerable and mortal. They are far from perfectly *like* the infinite Personhood of the Creator Being. But the *imperfection* of their likeness to God does not come from their being finite and being gifts, but *from their being passive*, and not purely active.

To be authentically finite is simply to be a creature in perfect likeness to God. Perfect creatures of God are finite, but they are not at all, as such, passive and dependent.

At the very moment of originative creation, those who perfectly received their beings *do not depend for their being* on God—nor on themselves and on one another. *They are not dependent at all*. They are persons who fully know and love God and their unique and perfect likeness to God, with which they were *purely endowed, sheerly gifted*.

Of all created persons, only we imperfect, self-crashed persons (demonic and human) are passive and dependent on God. Our fully or partially wrought independence *from* God paradoxically causes the dependency. But we take our obvious and often overwhelming condition of ontological dependency and assume it comes ultimately from God, not from us. We do not see that, while to depend is to be related, to be related is not *necessarily* to depend.

The necessary reason for our dependency in being we falsely attribute to God's causing us to be *out of nothing*. But being caused to *be* out of *nothing*—*by* an infinitely good and infinitely powerful Being—is grounds for inferring our *non-dependency*, transcending the categories of logic and "cosmologic" (ways of thinking about cosmological matters).

We refuse to consider that our obvious ontological dependency comes rather from our defective *ontological reception* of creation-causality. *By* our being, *for* our being, and *with* our being, we created our own chaos and dependency.

We cannot, *or will not*, consider that God's gifting of being *as being* is the very opposite kind of activity from the dependency-ridden causation in be-*coming* (being coming back to itself). Nevertheless, we should, at least, try to realize that God's activity is not a captive of the laws of logic and cosmologic. Nor should ours be—even now—totally so.

Whatever God does is not in the least dependency-rendering, since there is no dependency either within God or in "the *nothing*," from which or by which dependency could arise. In creating, God causes finite independence by the activity of infinite independence. God does not cause infinite being, but simply *independent, super-relational, finite* being.

The real *infinity* of God is missing in our notion of God's power of gifting creatures immaculately to be. To us in our cosmological frame of reference, God seems to be a magnificently powerful cause of dependent beings. We do not see God as a supreme Being independent of passivity-rendering conditions and dependency-rendering relationships. Moreover, we might *say* God is a Supreme Independent Being, but we do not seem to mean it *really*. At least unconsciously, we seem to require that God be subject to our "laws of dependence" in logic and cosmology.

Because every instance of cause-and-effect that we know in *this* world is a matter of the effect depending on the cause for its existence or for its coming to exist, we think that *that kind* of dependency must be at the heart of our *relationship* to God. But that kind of thinking is virtually criminal. A prime symptom of our step backward from our original being.

In our ontological arrogance, we think that God *must* create in essentially the same way we create—albeit with much more power. According to our ego-perspective, God must create beings that *depend on* the Creator—just as we create effects that depend on us. We do not entertain the prospect of our own beings as being-unique and originatively limited, yet *independent-with* the Creator.

The intrinsic effect of our refusal to *be fully* as we were gifted originally to be—*independent-with* God—is to render ourselves immediately somewhat *independent-of* (or *independent-from*) God. So, now we think and speak from the results of that free act of self-determination. In other words, we *caused* our independence-*from* God, and so we are now dependent *on* God to bring us back to our originative independence-*with*. Since *we* are dependent on God now for our power to come back to being as we were gifted (*independent-with* God) we think *every* created person—by being *created*—is like us in being dependent *on* God. We are thinking in denial.

Egocentrically, we suppose that since *we* have a necessarily *dependent* relation to God, so every created person must have one, too. (And we seem blind to the paradox of our own being as *both* dependent *and* not dependent on God.)

Our own being has locked itself out from itself and from its own deviant acts and misrepresentations. And this ontological-epistemic lockout of our own being—this spiritual *repression*—is, in many respects, almost total.

Within the covenant of creation, the results are tragic. Our either-or, univocal minds tend to fixate on *one* meaning for independence: "independence-*from*" or "independence-*of*." That common meaning is, of course, the opposite of "dependence on." We think then that things are *either* independent *or* dependent with respect to one another. We do not recognize that the heart of *being* and of ultimate created reality is a relationality of beings who are persons—gifted to be "independent-with" one another—thanks to God, the three *infinitely* Independent Persons Who created us.

Chapter 10

How Becoming Is Confused
with Being

Unconsciously, we take our cue from the world of becoming (being coming back to itself from a crash). We do not seem to realize that the whole cosmos is double-edged. This world of passive-reactive matter and motion is *both* the result of an ontological disaster within being *and* an effective assurance of the redemption in progress—of the redemptive remedy having been gifted to all self-afflicted persons.

Somehow believers know that the world of *energy-based* matter called the cosmos is a gift of redemptive creation. But few seem to have any idea about the willful catastrophe that must have originatively caused ("created") or occasioned this world. An ontological and spiritual "big bang" is existentially repressed in our spiritual depths.[24]

Nevertheless, we can still detect, in the present condition of cosmic matter, the redemptive and recuperative process. This world shows itself to be recovering by means of the dynamism of its remedial *forms* of matter and motion and by the *telic* character of all cosmic entities.

---

[24] The physical "big bang" of which science is presently so enamored might be considered a "spin off" of this originative "big bang."

Everything physical—human or otherwise—is ordered to the purpose of the redemption and salvation of fallen human persons. We insist nonetheless that God *must have* created the world basically as it is.

Apparently, we think God creates as we do, very imperfectly—despite the magnificence. We "talk a good game" about God being infinite in being and activity. But we think of God as, in effect, majestically finite in the very act of creating beings "*out of nothing*"—in the manner of a Maker of forms, instead of a true Creator of finite *being*.

The gift of *being*, however, is different from the gift of *becoming*. God gave both. The gift of *being* came "out of nothing." The gift of becoming came "out of something." This latter gift acts from within the beingful (ontological) remnants of the fractuality (fractured actuality) and of the void that was caused *by us* in failing to respond fully to the *gift of being*. We continue that failure even now.

By badly receiving that originative gift-being itself *who we are* personally, we caused ourselves both to implode and to explode, creating incredible energy. *Implosion* caused the *energy* of our personal bodily being to exist. *Explosion* caused, together with the explosions of multitudes of others' freedom, the energy of the cosmos at large. With infinite "patience," God works within both energies and within their passive-reactive matter, even becoming incarnate in the Person of Jesus Christ.

The gift of *becoming* is redemptive activity as operative in all human forms of recovery—cosmic, physical, emotional, mental, spiritual, sacramental, and so forth. *Becoming* is the world and work of Redemptive Creation.

Moreover, the gift of *being* is the effect of the originatively *giftive* activity of God that is infinitely powerful and causes us to *be* whole, perfect, free respondents to that very gift. *Being* as such is not a *world*; it does not *exist*. It does not "stand outside itself" (*ex-sistere*) in any way. *Being* simply and brilliantly *is*.

We failed—to one degree or another—to *receive* the gift of being. As a result, we both *are* and *exist*. We are both perfect and imperfect. As imperfect, we are opaque to ourselves and others. Paradoxically, our (imperfect) becoming and existence are transpiring *within* our perfect finite being. Our imperfection occurs right *within* our perfection.

We require the healing gift of becoming. And the heart of *personally effective* becoming is the radically receptive activity of *repentance*. This activity of sorrowing before God over our personal contribution to evil takes many forms, including forgiveness of self and others. Yet it does not come readily.

The very way we know empirical realities keeps us captive. Our defectively intellective *way of knowing*—a knowing proper to matters of space and time—includes typically moving from one dependent premise to another, and from such premises to a totally dependent conclusion. As a result, we seem to think that *all* of the *content* of this dependent *way of knowing* must likewise be essentially a matter of dependency. We think that not only every effect *has* a cause, but that every effect *depends* on its cause—after all, *we effects* surely do.

By assuming, however, that to cause is necessarily to render dependent we are not effectively—or, at least, not consciously—repenting of the *depths* of our sin. Only in a crashed and recovering creation, and among the recovering creatures themselves—recovering spiritually as well as physically—does causing *necessarily* entail dependency. The dependency-rendering kind of causing is involved in the struggle to recover some awareness of our "deep down" unique self. But this self, as an unconditional gift of God, is designed to be finitely independent-*with* God and *with* all of originative being.

Our present mode of dependency-ridden thinking, then, makes it quite difficult for us to see what we are looking at. From our typically fallen human way of *knowing through dependency,* we have to begin to discern our *being-with-being independence* that is the *core* (though not the only) *content* of this dependent kind of knowing.

In valid syllogistic reasoning, two premises cause a rational conclusion. But the obvious dependency of the conclusion readily serves to block within our minds the independence of some of the content of the knowing activity itself. Right within the rational knowing activity itself, there is the freedom of the intuitive intellect to know *what is essentially*—if not wholly—*independent* of the operations of our chronically-passive intellects.*

Unless we can see ourselves as independent-*with* other beings and distinguish this from the logic of dependency in which we are necessarily inured, we will continue to project our manner of dependent knowing onto the *originative* power of our knowing. We will miss the meaning of our *purely active* potencies to know and to love, gifted to us at the moment of creation.

In the meantime, we will continue to apply "the unmodified principle of causality" (every effect depends on its cause) not only to the whole of the created universe, but even to God and God's activity as well. We will regard God's act of causality, whereby we are brought to *be,* in fundamentally the same way as we regard God's other act of causality, whereby we are being redeemed from sin.

To cause someone to *be*, however, is not the same as to cause someone to *become*. Becoming is *always a more-or-less* kind of activity or effect, because self-wounded creatures are inherently involved. Being, however, is simply a total gift *to* someone *by* Someone, without any qualification.

God said, "Be." But we immediately and freely responded, "Maybe." We fractured our whole being by its own very first act. We thereby required reclamation. As it is now, we can refuse the recovery efforts of Infinite Love, even as we once, at least partly, declined to receive our originatively gifted actuality of being.

In truth, we are on trial in the world of *be*-coming, but never needed to *be* here. We could have fully and freely said *yes*, and there would have been nothing of us to *be-come*. We would have immaculately received our immaculately-gifted perfect (finite) *being*—doing so independently-*with* the infinitely perfect being of our gifting Creator.

Chapter 11

God Creates Beings
Who Create Themselves

The whole of the space-time universe is defective and laden with intrinsic dependencies in its every particle. Obviously, we human inhabitants are included among the massively dependent. This world of becoming could not be the *originative* world created by God.

Underlying the world of becoming is the proper sphere of *be*-ing. Therein the principal cause and the effects are *not* related as independent to dependent being, but as *infinitely independent* to *finitely independent* being.

Here again the "infinity factor" needs to be taken into account. Our difference from the Creator *originatively* is not between dependent being and independent being, but between *finitely* independent being and the *infinitely* independent Being. God creates finite *independent* beings, not finite dependent beings. God's infinite goodness and power graces every person with an independent and autonomous being.

An infinitely independent Being is "capable" only of creating completely "independent originals," who are not separative-from, but fully unitive-with, God. Originatively created persons are *not* brought to be as *united* with God—

whether wholly or partly. They are gifted to be as unit*ive*—ordered or structured to *be with* God. Each one, then, necessarily responds freely, and as a perfectly whole finite being, to this originative orientation.

Indeed, it is their *independence* in finite being that allows these created originals to defy their Creator totally, or to refuse partially their kind of being, or to affirm fully and gratefully the gift of being-at-all. Independence-*in* being is not the same as alienation or independence-*from*.

True independence *in* being makes it *possible* to *receive* the gift *fully*. If we were *essentially* and *originatively* dependent *in* being, we could never *receive fully*. How could we even *begin* to *receive*, as opposed to "being done to"? Heaven would be *impossible*.

Moreover, true recovery from sin only comes through restoration of a latent, pure independence-*with*. Conditions of both dependence on and independence-of or –from must be dissolved for the sake of *full interpersonal* communion.

No being that is *essentially dependent* on another being—with respect to being-at-all or with respect to anything else—can determine self *with respect to such a cause.* Snowflakes, flowers, and giraffes are beings of *essential* dependency; they are not essentially self-determining. They are effluents of our fractured freedom, fashioned by God to support our recovery.

But a human person *is*, in essence, self-determining. And *insofar as* we fallen humans would be, *in our very being*, merely *dependent on* someone or something we would be effectively unable to act freely *against*, or even to act truly *for* and *with*, this entity that is fundamentally other than we.[25]

Our originative relationship with God had to be a case of our being *independent-with* God—not *independent-of or – from*, nor *dependent-on*. However, we find this postulate difficult to understand or even to suppose, because we do not give God "infinite credit" for the love-gift of our created be-ing. The *infinity* of God is not being affirmed. And our "logic fixation" prevails.

Our servile minds result from our *originative* sin—a sin quite different from, yet correlative to, what has been known as *original* sin. Only our self-rifted minds could be satisfied with the common idea about God creating *ex nihilo* completely dependent beings. It requires incredibly complacent, passive minds, in order to think that way.

We assume falsely that *completely dependent* beings could either fully affirm or completely defy their infinitely independent Creator. But any measure of passivity or dependency precludes *full* freedom and intimacy.

If created persons were completely dependent on God, they would have to do their affirming or denying of God fully through the relationship in which they are being regarded as totally and exclusively *dependent*, namely, the relationship of being itself. The gift of be-ing that they receive would be thought to be necessarily dependent on God in its *be*-ing *activity*.

Instead, their being should be rightly considered to be *necessarily independent* and to be the unconditional *gift* of God, giving their being to itself. Our Creator's word,

---

[25] We are not even now *essentially* dependent on God. We are, because of our originative sin, *necessarily* dependent.

"Be," is essentially an act whereby a finite being is given to itself to be-*with* God.

Equally absurd is the implication that an exclusively dependent being could or would actually *love—in genuine freedom*—the infinitely independent Being. That would be parasitic love. Such "love" is *ultimately* a contradiction.

Dependent love is good and *necessary* for salvation. But if the love is authentically and remedially dependent within the person who is being redeemed, the person will be *also* exercising *personal independence*—by freely *willing* to depend on God for salvific grace. This practice of *willing* dependence will naturally lead to healing and to the fullness of a mutually independent kind of love— forever intended by God. Christians completely depend on the redemptive action of Christ by freely willing to receive it, right from the (independent) core of their sheerly-gifted being.

Confusion of the Ontological and the Moral

The usual way of distinguishing "what is moral" from what is ontological blocks the infinity of God from our consciousness. Perennially, we distinguish a relationship that is "intrinsically dependent" on God for being-at-all (ontological sphere) from our freedom of choice in the ways we live and behave (moral sphere).

But that distinction is overlayed with the affectations of linear logic. Overlooked is the real *being* we are talking about: the finite being that *does its own* gifted being. We *are* and *do* our own *unique* being. By our originative hesitation to be, we *maybe*-sayers have *created thereby*, in great part, our own spheres—reactive, yet redemptive— that are known as the physical, emotional, moral, and spiritual. Our very bodily manner of being, with all its attendant dimensions, is *both* a sign of the great crash that *we* caused *and* a sacrament of our personhood-in-recovery.

Moreover, the usual distinction between the ontological and the moral begs the question of "which came first" in our own being: the giving or the receiving. The answer is: neither.

God creates us whole and all at once: as persons, both giftive and receptive. Giftive means disposed essentially to give self to self and to all others. Receptive means disposed essentially to receive all that is—all truth—from God, self, and all others.

God's act of saying *BE* is so absolute and definitive that if, contrary to possibility, God were to cease *being—or even just knowing us*—we would go right on being. Our gifted finite *being* is perfect in its giftedness, if not in its receptedness. The traditional idea that if God "stopped knowing us" we would be annihilated is based on the assumption that our relationship to God is not only dependency for salvation, but dependency for being. God's *infinite* power and goodness of gifting *being* is virtually denied.

Creation is exclusively an *act of God*. But "being created" is entirely an *act of the created person*, who *receives* being by the *act itself of* that gifted being. By immediately and freely *receiving* personal being, the finite person creates the *receiving* of self *as* thus *also a giving* of self to self and to all others (including God), for better or worse, for best or worst.[26]

By way of *active receptivity*, the created person *creates* a self-destiny. From his or her purely active *power to*

---

[26] "Better or worse" is the *maybe* condition. "Best" is the total *yes* condition. "Worst" is the total *no* condition.

receive, three different kinds of *act* can be elicited: purely active affirming of being and of God, purely active deformation of self and others, or, in our case, impurely active affirmation that requires redemption.

On the one hand, as *God's* act, originative creation is a totally independent act—*depending* on nothing and no one, *not even on God*. (Our menial minds, of course, might falsely attribute to God's activity a dependency-on-God, as well as a *dependency-rendering* character.) The originative creating act, like all of God's infinite acts, is infinitely free and that means independent-*with* Self-and-others—not dependent on Self and others.

On the other hand, in total *likeness* to God, created persons who *fully receive and give* their very own gifted being thereby confirm their being as willing to be independent-*with* God—as *finitely* independent-*with* God. These perfectly receiving persons—whether angelic or human—receive their unique being by freely *doing* their own being *as* gifted. And that very receiving is (or involves) a spontaneously free giving of self to God and to the whole of creation. It is all done in one finite, *pure* act.

Infinite Being is *independent-with* whatever being there is, including Self and others. Finite (whole person) being is likewise *independent-with* whatever being there is, including self and others. The two prime kinds of being differ in their *kind* of relational independence—infinite and finite respectively.

But *dependent* being is really an *ill-received independent finite* being. Dependent being is in need of other being *in order to come to be* the perfect being it was gifted to be. Such is our plight in the cosmos wherein there is vast alienation from God and creatures—here in the backwaters of creation.

Our present, dynamic condition indicates, however, that our *existence*—our "cast out" kind of being—is being-coming-back to itself: be-*coming*. All dependent *persons*, if they are to "come back" to themselves, are going to have to come back eventually to their gifted being as independent-*with* God and independent-*with* every other being that wills likewise.

Paradoxically, however, this means that, granted our dependent condition, *we need to become completely dependent morally* and *spiritually* on God. Only by our doing so can God's infinite love free us back confluently into our originatively gifted way of *being*—being finitely independent-*with* ourselves, God, and all others.

We are called, above all, to become dependent morally and spiritually on God. But we can only *do* this real, live depending by exercising our personal will *independently* —not dependently. We have to be *willing* to be dependent.

There are, as it were, two dimensions or "directions" to our willing. One is vertical, so to speak, having to do with our immediate relationship to God and all being. The other is horizontal, having to do with our everyday decisions, large and small, made in this world of becoming. In the "vertical realm" willing is independently ours to do. In the "horizontal realm," willing depends on circumstances and moral conditions, as well as on the disposition of our "vertical," independent will.

We *independently will* ourselves (vertically) to be willfully *dependent* (horizontally) on God's means for salvation. We *do not dependently will* ourselves to be *dependent*. The self-determination to-*be*-saved-by-God is *ours* to do, not God's. While only God can do the saving, we must be *willing*. God cannot force our will nor do our willing for us. We are necessarily independent in being and in originative willing *power*.

We *maybe*-sayers need to undertake *freely* to be truly *dependent* on God. The free undertaking comes directly from our *agent will*, the purely active potency to will and love that the whole of our tradition in the West has repressed.[27]

But this *becoming* of our dependent beings should not be confused with our *being*. Underlying the condition of our dependence, we are actively grounded in God's absolute, originative gift to us: created independence in (and with) being. The rightful attention that we give to our *moral* relationship with God and with all others *should not substitute for* critically needed devotion to our being-*with*-being relationships, *underlying* our moral, passive-reactive condition of being.

Moral activity—both positive and negative—is an attempt to relate creatively from within our largely passive-reactive condition of being. In effect, our moral acts of conformity to natural and supernatural law should minister to our actively ontological independence-*with* God and all others.

God creates whole beings out of nothing. And these persons create their destiny out of something: out of the finitely magnificent being with which God *gifted* them.

---

[27] Aristotle discovered agent intellect. With him, many philosophers have recognized this power as a preconditioning light for any intellective knowing done in this world. But they have repressed its being a power to *know* as well—to know by purely active intuition. Agent intellect was, nonetheless, recognized as a most Godlike power, a pure act of intelligibility.

No "matching" *a priori* power of willing or loving was recognized. The agent will* was totally repressed...by that power of will itself. Agent will is so powerful that it can and has repressed itself "out of existence," so to speak. But not out of *being*.

Chapter 12

The Beingful Meaning of Independence

We are called to enter a new level in understanding *being*. The perspective of *being* as *essentially interpersonal* might even afford leverage for a deeper appreciation of the meaning of Revelation.

Scriptural Revelation, for instance, might be said to be *reportorial* in its basic nature. It *reports*, literally and figuratively, much of what we could not know by even the best forays of unaided reason into sacred history and its meaning. It also declares and proclaims. Our Scripture is telling us to read at least some of the texts with a particular kind of *response*. Is not Holy Scripture addressing us *interpersonally*?

We might begin to wonder whether we are being asked, by the whole of the text, to say we are sorry for having had to receive revelation at all. Why are we in the ontological position of having to know by *special revelation*? We must have caused the need, in the first place. Our side of the interpersonal relationship inherent in the Scriptures could be to *admit our part* in living out a revelational existence.

Scriptural Revelation's character—historical, directive, and descriptive—might really be demanding an admission from us. An explicit account of our originative ill-reception of be-ing might be intentionally missing from the writings of Scripture. Perhaps the truth of originative sin must come freely as an admission *from us personally*, and not simply as another report or declaration.

If we were to acknowledge our personal failure to receive our being fully, we could begin to read Revelation at a new level of meaning—more proportionately aware of our be-ing as originatively independent-*with* God. Implicit or explicit acknowledgement of sin at the heart of our created relations must come *freely* from us.

But we are absorbed by our early habits of thinking. Even great philosophers and theologians, like Thomas Aquinas, are at least "half-stuck" at the cosmological level. They use conceptualizations proper to studying the cosmos philosophically and then transfer them, virtually whole, to their analyses in the light of Revelation. That is why they see no problem in thinking that God created basically passive beings, like trees and water drops, directly *out of nothing*. They treat infinite activity *implicitly* as though it were not only mystery, but magic.

Other thinkers have offered, for the study of being, philosophical remedies that have yielded a *dichotomy* between the structure of matter (the cosmological) and the structure of being (the ontological). They regard abstract and formal entities as the only "really real." But *being* as such is neither material nor spiritual. Such classifications tend to play off one kind of being against the other, dimming the light.

Nevertheless, *being as being is basically interpersonal*. Purely to be is to be a person, transcending, while including in the case of the human, the categories of matter and spirit. The latter arise *as categories* in fallen human consciousness "after" the originative sin.

As mentioned, our *ultimate* ontological interrelationship with our Creator is one of independence, not dependence. Otherwise, we would all be latent pantheists, believing that, when all is said and done, we are part of God, the *only* independent kind of being. Unconsciously, we would be considered, in effect, *parts* of that one *independent* being.

In our empirical world, we unwittingly covet our cozy thinking of God as a *co-dependent* in the midst of our self-aholic addictions. We shrink from being co-*independent* with God. Being independent-*with* God gives us a mortal fright. We somehow suspect that if we would be independent-*with* God, we would be totally responsible for all our activity, including especially our activity that relates us essentially to God: our activity of *be*-ing, of *do*-ing our *being*.

But that is the point. To be independent-*with* is grace-full being. God's grace is the gift of friendship* such that we are being-*with*…not simply being *for* or *toward*.

Our being-based activity is ordinarily unrecognized by us, but it is being done in a spiritually unconscious way by our repressed *agent* intellect and *agent* will. This hidden receiving of our originatively gifted being transpires, even as this being now lamely struggles for salvation.

We co-acted with God, at the moment of creation *ex nihilo*, to constitute a basic ontological structure. Our failing reception "created" a structural deficiency in that relationship and in our own being. So, our moral activities in this fallen world are all about how to relate well with our co-ontological structure and our human nature. Tragically, this "co" (relation with God) is not recognized as ontology-affecting, as affecting the structure of our *be*-

ing. We have repressed this dimension on account of shame over our originative sin.

We live in a passive-reactive condition of being, springing from our self-wrought dependency. And we seem to regard our very being as God's *product*, rather than God's *sheer gift of freedom*.

Where Dependency First Enters Being

Dependency in being does *not* come from God in any way. Dependency does *not* come by God's activities— especially not by the act of creation *ex nihilo*. Dependency comes from the way God's creating activity is *received* by some creatures—the *maybe* ones and the *no* ones.

By their first activity—one that was necessarily fully free and untempted—multitudes of angelic persons, and at least billions of human persons, received their being badly.

Angelic *no*-sayers entered their dependency on God by *willing* to be fully independent-*of* God—and thus fully *dependent* on themselves. *Paradoxically*, this bad act of will—of ontological self-determination—made them totally dependent on God, but in a manner that locked out any redemptive prospect. They said *no* with their whole being, without the slightest shadow of a *yes*. They caused or created their hell forever. Likewise, there might have been some fully *no*-saying *human* persons causing their own everlasting frustration.

At the moment they received their originative creation, humans who were *maybe*-sayers entered their dependency on God by *willing* to be *partly* independent-*of* God—and thus largely dependent on themselves. This ontological condition made them decisively dependent on God, but in a manner that held out hope for redemption, due to the partial *yes* in their originative response to the gift of being and to God.

Dependency Weighs Down Relationships

Originative sin created dependency. Our relationships with God and one another were critically wounded and they are in need of mega-healing. The divine effort of redemption and salvation likewise began at that same originative moment.

Eventually, through our being conceived, born, and developed in space and time, we *maybe*-sayers can become awakened to our own being. But then, having originatively twisted the reality of our being, we inevitably start to think about *all reality*—including the *yes*-sayers and the beatified—in terms of one person being dependent on others, *just as we have made ourselves to be.* (Projection is the hallmark of self-centered knowers).

Dependent persons, like us, confuse relationships with dependencies. We think that to be related is to be dependent because all of our *empirically* recognizable relationships are dependent ones. Only careful ontological reflection brings us eventually to understand that to *relate* is not necessarily to *depend.*

The life of the Triune God and of the interrelationships of the blessed in heaven are perfect examples of relating without depending. But even healthy, loving friendships on earth contain a core of shared or mutual independence, in the midst of a multitude of attendant dependencies. We can become aware of this truth by contemplating the affirming kind of love, from which friendship radiates.

Chapter 13

An Affirming Kind of Love

Good human relationships are based on the attitude of sharing. They do not necessarily signify dependency. Love is their primary purpose.

Love promises communal independence. A true lover always creates less dependency for the beloved. The more the loved person is authentically free and independent, the more this person becomes *capable* of intimacy. The less independence, the less ability to unite freely with others.

The Main Meaning of Love

There are various kinds and levels of love. But we might entertain one central meaning for all loves, including the human, the angelic, and the divine. At its core, *love* is the activity of willing the truest and best for self and all others, especially God, despite the cost.* This meaning for love is common to God and created persons. God's love involved *immeasurable cost* by means of the incarnation, passion, and death of God the Word.

On our part, love comes in *degrees.* Degrees of *willingness.* To the degree that one *wills*—not just wishes or wants—the truest and best for all, one can be said to be loving. And, of course, God's *willing* of the truest and best for all is unlimited.

Moreover, at any given moment, each created person loves everyone to the same degree. I cannot *love* my closest friends any more *intensely* than I really love, or *will* the best for, my worst enemy. I *like* my friends with a richness far greater than that which I have with my acquaintances or with folks I have never met. But I do not *love* them more intensely.

Anyone can take the "test." Think of the person in this world whom you love least. That is the degree to which you *love* God, yourself, and everyone else. Love is not friendship, but it is the necessary core for genuinely sharing relationships.

Friendship is not just companionship or buddyhood. Friendship consists in loving *plus liking*. We become more or less friends by the human goods we share and the depth to which the sharing goes. But, when I increase or decrease my *liking* for someone, I do not *love* more or less than before.

Love is a precondition for genuine friendship. Increasing love means increasing my *ability* to be an authentic friend with anyone. But love is not the same as friendship. I can love people without our sharing anything of particular meaning and value.

When we consider the *kind* of causality that *loving* is— even finite loving—we are called to think differently from the usual. In our better moments, we might recognize that the love of friendship and the giving and receiving—not the same as "give and take"—in relationships of genuine love are *essentially* free of dependency.

Although it is created activity, the kind of causality that is exercised by *pure finite acts* of being is not dependency-rendering. The good angels and any humans, for instance, who did not sin originatively share in one another's unique independence and freedom. By totally loving activity, the created person gives love without rendering the recipient dependent. The loved one is thereby free to act independently, while receiving the lover's gift of purely affirming love.

In this *affirming kind of love*, the loved one is *gifted* to himself or herself, spontaneously from the heart of the lover. There is no hesitation. The loved one knows this gifting and feels the goodness of his or her unique self in the presence of the loving one. We might ask ourselves whether there is anyone in our lives who treats us spontaneously as delightful in our very *being-who-we-are*. The incomparable gift of affirmation.

The act of affirming love takes myriad forms, but it always unpossessively delights in the unique personhood of the loved one. In the light of the affirming kind of love, the loved one knows and feels special and privileged to *be* and to be *this person who he or she is*.

There are many unaffirmed people here in the world of *becoming*. They know themselves without feeling affirmed. They have never been truly loved for who and what they are. They have not experienced the warmth of another—family member, relative, or friend—who really delights in their *being*, far beyond merely 'functional friendship.'

Unaffirmed people need to prepare themselves to recognize and to receive such affirming love from someone who spontaneously says, in effect, *yes*, you are good and I like being with you. Words need not be spoken. Attitudes are critical.

Unaffirmed people have been born physically, but not really emotionally. They are quite deprived of the gift of affirmation.* They long for love—secretly or openly—as a second birth.[28] They need an emotional birth, a second birth that would free them for warmth in human relationships. But, now in our fallen condition, this birthing must be done by *another*. The needy one cannot give emotional birth to self.

Besides, all of us need to receive—not just to undergo—a third birth, a supernatural one, through receiving sacraments and myriad other helps of divine grace.

God is the *infinitely affirming lover*. God creates other (finite) potentially affirming lovers who are capable of pure, unpassivized loving. God gifts them totally to themselves. *Essential* love, even among created persons, *is not* passive or dependent or self-centered. Nor does real love *cause* the dependencies that abound in ordinary human existence.

The *affirming kind* of love among creatures is like the covenant of creation. Absolutely *giftive*. The *attitude of the lover is* one of giving the loved one to himself or herself. *Not* so much in giving self to the other (*agape*) or in giving the other to self (*eros*). Nor even self and other sharing, as in *phillia*. By a mutually affirming love, the

---

[28] See Conrad Baars, *Born Only Once:The Miracle of Affirmation* (Quincy, Ill.: Franciscan Press, 2001). Affirmation psychology comes from the genius of two psychiatrists, Anna Terruwe and Conrad Baars. Their largely clinical perspective on affirming love is remarkably open to vast spiritual and ontological ramification. They tell of a talk on affirmational love that they gave to Bishops attending a Synod, meeting in Rome in 1971. Only one Bishop approached them immediately after the presentation: Karol Wojtyla of Krakow, who later became Pope John Paul II. The talk was revised by Baars and published by Franciscan Herald Press in 1973, as "How to Treat and Prevent the Crisis in the Priesthood."

lover and beloved are gifted as independently-*with* each other. At the *heart* of this love, there is no dependency, as there is in the other kinds of love, where one or both parties exhibit dependency.[29]

Locking Out Love

There is no other source through which dependency *can first arise* than through creatures forsaking, willfully and untemptedly, their prime relationship with God. These fallen creatures create their own orginative dependency. Thus, their (subsequent) moral relationship can only modify, that is, add to or subtract from, this originative dependency.

From the beginning of reflective history to the present, thinkers have overlooked the reality of originative sin. This failure keeps us blocked, and locked out, from the *heart* of our originative *inter-relationship* with God, and from the *core* of our need for a personal Savior.

The passive-reactive intellect, the base of the ordinary work of understanding, has been characterized in the tradition as a *tabula rasa* (a blank slate). By this intellect, thinkers have often featured the relationship between God and creatures as a one-way street, with creatures being related to God, but God not being related to creatures. The *predicamental* notion of "relation" holds sway by a kind of "logic lock." The relationship is construed as dependency, such that God, who is independent, is not "related" to us in that sense. Such a grandiose case of univocal thinking then impedes, if not blocks, awareness of the intrinsically interpersonal relationship of being *with* being.

---

[29] Affirming love is central to all the loves. For instance, the famous "four loves" of C. S. Lewis are like fingers of the hand of love, of which affirmational love would be the palm.

The distinction between being-related and being-dependent *cannot be made* by a *passively* based intellect that takes itself too seriously. So, we have been suffering silently. We have identified our passivity with our being-created, instead of realizing that the passivity did not come from our finitude, but from our originative deficiency of love—our *freely distorted response to* our own finitude. Originatively, we failed to be freely, freshly, and fully affirming of ourselves. As a result, we are even *cast out* about *being* "cast out."

Friendship and the Base of the Blame Game

All human relationships in passive matter and motion do involve dependencies of myriad kinds. But, despite inclusion of kinds of love that are based on dependencies, the *love* of a friend for a friend is, at its heart, a gift of being "independent-with" the friend. Love at the core of friendship does not render the other in the least dependent, but rather disposes the friend to be more independent-*with* self and others.

By reflecting on the love at the heart of genuine friendships, we can intuit the likeness of God's covenant of creation. In that pristine covenant, created persons are given (*ex nihilo*) wholly to themselves and are gifted with an immediate ontological power to be-*with* the Uncreated Persons of the divinity.

We might regard it as intolerable to think that God could create *independent beings* and to give the total power of destiny to the very *being* of a "mere creature." Nonetheless, God's infinitely affirming kind of love demands the independence of truly shared relationships.

We assume that "being and activity" are not only quite different, but separable. The notion of a separation between my being or even my "being here" and what I do *with* it and *about* it assumes that my *being* is something that God "does for me"—and even *to* me—while my *acts* might somehow be mine to do. My acts, then, amount to *reacts*: reactions to what was *done to* me.

The traditional idea seems to be that I do my own *activity* on the basis of what I have been given by God, but that I do not really *do* my *being*. I simply respond to the gift (the package of powers?) by doing whatever I choose to do under its constraints.

Such thinking fails to acknowledge the reality that my being is something *only I* can *do*—not God, nor anyone else. The whole of the *gift* is *who I am and who I co-create myself to be*. Hence this very being is the ultimate in *my* freedom to be, to co-create with God, and to live. Since I am not living so well right now—living here in a world where bad things happen to good people—there is no one to blame for the essence of that condition but myself.

Nevertheless, I surely am inclined to try to blame others, such as Adam and Eve and Satan consciously, and God unconsciously. In that way, I afford myself a major means to escape having to face my primal affront to Love—an offense that caused me to be *existent* in a world where bad things happen to people, "good and bad." The implicit or explicit *attitude* of blaming is not an affirming kind of love for either friends or enemies.

Dis-Affirmation in the Midst of Love

Finiteness of being does not come from passivity—nor in conjunction with it. Dependency, however, does come from passivity.

By failing to exercise *fully* the finite, purely active potency to be and do, with which I was originatively gifted, I created the passive potency by which my being is now enfeebled. Even the Incarnate Son of God was laden—unjustly—with this passivity in the process of *be-coming* our Redeemer.

And passivity does *not* come ultimately from activity, especially not infinite activity. Passivity can only result from *actual resistance* to the infinite goodness and power of the Person(s) of infinitely pure act.

This reserve—reticence to be—is the self-determination of each of those created persons like us who said *maybe*: maybe I will receive fully my being as God's sheer gift, maybe I will not. That *maybe response* was itself an ill-reception of who I am. That very response created my dependency.

Such an ontologically hesitant *yes-no* to our being was a partial denial of the *goodness* of being. By that denial, we must have absolutely shocked our own being. The shock would have been so totally traumatic that we buried it alive in the depths of our being. It would have created an ontological crater, now known as the unconscious. This dark spiritual chasm or void is taking its daily toll on our physical, psychic, and spiritual lives.

We are human persons in recovery, who are both finite and defective in our freely self-wrought—now spiritually unconscious—condition of being. If we had said fully and freely *yes*, we would be solely pure acts of finite, ecstatic love of God, of ourselves, and of all others—as we were gifted to be. If we would have said simply *yes*, there would be no passivity in our perfect finite gift of being and of being-who-we-are; and so there would be no dependency either on ourselves and other creatures or on God. There would be only mutually affirming love—God affirming us, we affirming God.

Our relationships would be pure and secure by being *fully* active—from the heart of our being. Our being would be an *unconditional gift of love*, that we fully and gratefully received, without any question of passivity or dependency.

We might find ourselves resisting this realization. But our reluctance could be coming from the cosmological fog that prevents us from seeing clearly the essential difference between the effects of creation *ex nihilo* (celebrative creation) and the effects of creation *ex aliquo* (redemptive creation). When attending to the activities of originative being, we are laboring under a massive unwillingness to let go of our two-valued, linear, and necessarily servile logic. By such unwillingness we are hiding aplenty.

The passivity underlying linear logic is the condition for major self-deceptions. Our fixation on univocal logic works devotedly in the service of passivity-based understanding. As a result, we misunderstand the freedom of love.

Another consequence is the misunderstanding of evil, to which we now turn.

Chapter 14

The Meaning of Evil

In Christian teaching, evil has a perennial definition. Evil is considered to be the privation *of*, or *in*, the goodness of someone or something. Evil is the absence of what ought to be.

When generalized, evil is often thought to be not *really* real. St. Thomas Aquinas famously treats of the blindness in a blind person as not real *being*, because it is a deprivation or privation in a substance, and not itself something substantial. In the distinction between real and logical being, evil tends to fall on the logical side.

Latent in such a distinction seems to be the assumption that to be is necessarily to be a substance. This Aristotelian bearing on being is highlighted in scholastic philosophy. St. Thomas says that an accident* is *"magis entis quam ens"* (more *of* a being than a being). So, if an accident—such as the green of a leaf or the smoothness of skin or the vibrance of a personality—is not so much a being as *"of* a being," then surely evil, a 'negative accident,' is thought to be even less real.

The Aristotelian meaning for being *as substance* seems to be ruling much of traditional philosophy and theology in the West. Along with other metaphysical short sights about being, this idea locks us out of real knowledge of our *originative* sin: the very origin of evil in our lives. It makes it difficult to take evil as seriously as it *really is*.

Even when we are afflicted by atrocities, we are pressed to think of them as not really real—as not having "full being" or "adequate being." The reality of moral evil is thought to consist in the privation of good will by the agents of these injustices.

In that idea there is much truth. But the physical and moral bad effects on the victims receive relatively short shrift, even as the blindness of the blind one seems to be relatively discounted. After all, so it can be assumed, God is not much offended by simply physical evils.

This rendition of meaning exemplifies the failure to distinguish being as known in and through cosmocentric thinking from being as known through person-centered thinking.

St. Thomas quite well observed that only persons are *being* in the full sense. Only persons are gifted with intellect and will, the specific powers to receive their own being and to receive the being of their gifting Creator, as gifting. But St. Thomas did not "follow through" in his insight and apply it to creation *ex nihilo* and to other features of reality.

Nonetheless, the consequences for weakness of meaning are great. Persons are said to be *being* in the full sense. But evil is thought *ultimately* to arise only from intents and actions in this world of real, but moderate consciousness. (Vicious animal attacks are not considered to be evil in the moral sense, because they do not emanate specifically from persons. Physical evils, such as hurricanes and volcanoes, are not just distinguished, but separated, from moral evils. In not a few contexts, they are thought to be "acts of God.") The full measure of a person as a complete being is overlooked.

Evil as Positively Ontological

We only need to look outside of our logic lock.[30] Then we can see that specifically human acts and intentions can actually be *positively* evil or ontological positives *as evil*. They are not *merely* privations or impotencies of will. Behind the moral deprivational disposition is an originative will act, solely of the agent, that creates a really, if partially, distorted structure in the agent's receiving of being. That malreception is real being, not merely logical or second intentional being.

Human acts of ill will, like angelic ones, are ontological challenges to God, not merely moral distortions. They bring into being—without God's "help"—something real that can last forever. They represent the structure of persons, receiving their being in ontological—not just moral—defiance of God. Within their gifted-by-God-substance, human sins cause a deconstruction of the

---

[30] Our destiny is not with Faith and logic, but with Faith and reason. Reason and logic, however, are often conflated. Reason transcends logic right from within it, even as Faith transcends reason. *Reason* is our natural power to see, in reality independent of ourselves, relationships proportionately (*ratio*)—creature to creature and creature to Creator, *etc*. *Logic* is the art of correct thinking that has been largely denatured into dealing with the thoroughly disproportionate machinations of mind about passive matter.

Anyone, for instance, who wishes to think about angels or God proportionately, that is, rationally is going to have to transcend the linear notion of thinking that serves ordinary egocentric purposes. Knowing mainly for the sake of *what is known*, and for union with it, belongs to reason. Logic, however, stripped from reason, can be forced into the service of knowing mainly for the sake of the *knower*. Logic is, then, used mainly in the service of the knower and only secondarily, perhaps, in the service of the truth. The meaning for logic today—whether of common sense, of the natural logic of the human mind as in Aristotle, or of mathematical and symbolical character—remains far from its etymological roots in *logos* and in the Word of God.

receptive side of their *being*—a flaw or fall that was not intended by God, but is very real nonetheless.

As it is now, under the ontological shortsights about evil and the *being* of evil, we tend to judge even moral evils, such as coolly deliberated murder or rape, as deprivations in the human wills of their perpetrators. They certainly are that. But we fail to recognize their character as positively, if partly, restructuring the *being* and the *personhood* of their agents. By originative sinning, these persons have partly—or totally, in the case of demons—deconstructed their receptivity to *being*. And they act it out in immoral behaviors.

We do not see that moral evils are not only defacements of the agents' relations with other created persons, but that these evils also come from their relations with God. God *is* mocked, really offended. And if God is *really* offended, the offense or evil is really real.

Sin is just as real for the being of the offender or evil doer as any good done by a virtuous person. If morally positive acts are *really* good determinations of their agents, morally negative acts are *really* bad determinations of their agents.

Evil is real, and *positively* a *negative*. Not good. But positively *real*. Evil is not just an absence of a due good, but also the *presence* of an anti-good. This thought is not Manichean. It has nothing to do with an 'Evil Substance divinity.' There is no such thing as *an evil substance as gifted by God*; but there is such a thing as an *evil substance as self-disreceived* by a created person, such as Lucifer and so many others, including ourselves in part.

We require deeper insight into paradoxes. We need to see that created persons, such as multitudes of angels and humans, who were evil-*doing* at the moment of creation *ex nihilo*, create for themselves and for all reality a destructure of their capacity to receive being. That distortion is just as "positive" and *real* as any moral or ontological good. [Just ask any demon in hell whether this (distorted) condition is real. And while you are at it, ask any blind person on earth, "Is blindness real?"] In many cases, this destructurization *lasts forever*. That is real. Real *be*-ing. Real *be*-ing *hostile* to the good. Philosophers and theologians are missing the elephant in the living room.

Evil as Not Really Serious

Thinkers in the Christian tradition have not taken the *interpersonal* character of being *as being* sufficiently into account. They continue to rely—unconsciously for the most part—on an undifferentiated view of creation, wherein the creation *ex nihilo* (out of nothing) is virtually eclipsed by the creation *ex aliquo* (out of something).

Church doctrine is expressed, for instance, in the quite true claim that a primeval event at the beginning of the history of humankind caused the fall of all from grace. But that fall is in the line of history and does not deal with *why* history was needed in the first place. The sin of Adam was critical historywise as the origin of evil in our becoming, but could hardly be decisive for the origin of evil in our *being,*

Why was history itself needed? God is infinitely good *and infinitely powerful*. So, the original sin of one or more human *persons* could not contaminate the *being* of multitudes of others without each one having been self-contaminated, thereby rendering the self vulnerable to the original sin. Hence, a divine healing ministry is required *by means of* space, time, and history.[31]

Again, because we are missing insight into the real *infinity* of God, we think that evil is not a "positive" reality. We have effectively denied the infinity of God and substituted for infinity expressions such as "all-good, all-powerful," "fullness of Being," and others. So, we have "reason" to tend toward denying the reality of evil by calling it a mere privation of what is good and not a positive "contribution" (*no*-saying) to being or reality. Evil is considered as not really real, because unconsciously it is not taken as offending *really infinite* Being. The infinity of God and the meaning of freedom, created and uncreated, suffer terribly.

Evil and the Transcendentals

The miss-take on evil shows where the classical tradition of the transcendental characteristics of being can be

---

[31] The Immaculate Conception is a case in point. In the *new* theistic view, our inheritance of *original* sin is inevitable because, by our commission of *originative* sin, we deserved it.

At the moment of creation *ex nihilo*, we sinned *with* Adam and multitudes of others. Infinite freedom is infinite love, but it is not at all arbitrary. God cannot *exempt* anyone from personal sin. God can and does *forgive* sin, but could not really exempt anyone from *personal* sin, and still be the God of freedom, of love and responsibility. As co-Redemptrix, Mary, the mother of Jesus, must have been one of those humans who said fully *yes* at the moment of creation—as well as at the temporal moment in Nazareth. No '*prevention* of inheritance' was really needed. The "prevention rationale" of Scotus is understandable and logical in its own right, but lacks roots. Mary's originative full *yes* to God and to her being was enough to preserve her, like her Son, from any personal evil. No need for the kind of reasoning ("*creatio ex machina*") offered by Duns Scotus and others.

Every prebirth baby and toddler is a full person, crashed, and reaching, placental-like, for salvation from both originative and original sin. Each one is susceptible to death and to meeting God with the character and the consequences of his or her originative sin. The originative act of *maybe*-saying landed this magnificent, angel-like person, now as a "little person," in the world of redemptive creation, and at a particular point on the continuum of *yes* and *no* through the exercise of first, purely active freedom.

improved. This metaphysical orientation includes the idea that to be is to be good, true, one, beautiful, and so on. God creates only insofar as someone (or something) is true, good, and beautiful. This leaves little room for saying that to be ugly is to be, to be evil is to be, and to be false is to be. The God of this metaphysics (cosmogenic, as it is) is something of a tyrant, not letting evil *really be*.

To the contrary, "to be" is *not necessarily* to be good. While there could not be *any* evil if there were not goodness, "to be" could be to be bad. Not wholly so, of course, for God is the supreme cause of every being's substance as gifted (though *not as received*). The created person is gifted by God to receive his or her be-ing *by that being* itself.

Failure to realize that each created person is a pure act of finite being as gifted by God, causes theologians to treat our first act of freedom as a *moral* act—an act that is done "after" receiving our being, not in it and by it—not mainly an *ontological act*. That *we* can really *do* being is not acknowledged.

We, then, overlook the reality of *our receiving act* of being. We fail to recognize it as something that we and we alone *do*. That act is both a perfect gift to us from God *and* also an act that we are and do in likeness to God. We do not merely "have" our being (*habens esse*), we *are* our being. And we do our own being; God *cannot* do it *for us*. God does God's *infinite act* of Being; we do our *finite* acts of being.

Both good and evil are *really real*. They affect the very structure of the substance of individual personhood.

Chapter 15

The Cause of Evil

God, the Supreme Being, is known as the uncaused cause of all else that is. But evil really *is*. (The survivors of a holocaust, or even of a tsunami, can serve as witnesses.)

Is God then the supreme, if not the specific, cause of evil? Is God the uncaused cause of evil?

Not really. According to traditional theology, evil is a privation *in* things and not a thing or "a being" in itself. So, evil is, as it were, a moral "accident." Evil is caused specifically by the ill-willing of finite persons, who are responsible for how they exercise the supreme gift of the being and of the freedom that they receive from God.[32]

---

[32] *Cause* here must be defined as that upon which something depends for its being or its coming to be. Such is the definition of a cause in this world. Unfortunately, it has been taken perennially to be the meaning for cause when applied to God's act of creating us out of nothing. But "nothing could be further from the truth."

As Creator of being "out of nothing" God does not stamp us or determine us to be this way or that way and thus dependent in being. God gifts us with our own act of being and of freedom. God creates our *kind* of being (essence): our being both *human* and *this* unique human. We have a common essence and a unique, personal essence—the person, Jane, has both humanity and Janeness. And we *independently* create the kind of *unique, relational human* being we *will* to be. We do not create our kind of being essentially: human, rather than angel, dog, flower, *etc.*, nor our unique identity as *this* person But, by our gifted ontological freedom to receive, we do create the kind of destiny that *we will* to attain. We will to *be* that destiny. (Continued, next page.)

God is not then the uncaused cause of *all* being. Created persons, not God, cause their own evil, as well as their own virtues. However little or much it is, the evil *and good* that we do is *ours*—our doing, not God's.

We are gifted with the *power* to do only good: finite good. But we are *able* to do bad. The acts and habits of the exercise of our perfect power to do good are strictly ours: not those of God, nor of angels, nor of other humans.

Moreover, God is not the uncaused cause of God. In the Trinity of Divine Persons, according to Christian thought, the One Person does not *cause* the others. They *are* eternally: without beginning or end. There is no cause for God.

As delineated earlier, God's causing us to be *ex nihilo* is a distinct *kind* of causality that could be called *gifting*, rather than causing, since it entails no dependency of the effect on the cause. We may think of it in terms of dependency, because of the passivity of our cosmocentric minds.

But, in the question about the Persons of the Trinity proceeding from one another, there is no *ex nihilo* and no "ex" at all. So, the infinite gifting involved does not qualify as causing. Yet the likeness of the creation *ex nihilo* of finite persons to the Triune procession is magnificent. We are like the Persons of God in being gifted, although our being gifted is a causal one.

But God does not in any way *cause*, much less "gift," evil. In creation *out of nothing*, God's gift to us is the *freedom to be and do who we are of our own will*, as independent-*with* God and all created persons. That we

---

The causality of creation is a gifting without totalistic determining. We are free to be as we *will* to be, thanks to God the Gifter. No strings are attached.

were *able* to abuse our freedom is necessary to that freedom itself as finite. Being *unable* to abuse the power of freedom would make us unfree, automatons of God. Quite un-Godlike.

Evil is caused by finite persons abusing the gift of freedom-to-be-who-they-are by means of their own will. Indeed, by means of their own being. The virtuous acts of a finite person—as well as the vicious acts of one who freely goes against God's gift of being who he or she is—are caused by that person. And not by God. God cannot *do* our acts *for us* without taking away our freedom. But God can and does gift and support *infinitely*—without limits—*our* being and *our* freedom to *be* and *do* who we are.

If we do our own free acts of willing and choosing—to one decisive extent or another, with more or less free volition—then we are the *supreme* cause of *these* acts as their totally adequate agency. God is necessary that we be, and be who and what we are; but we are necessary as free agents to know and love what we are *willing* to know and love. God can do nothing of our knowing and loving, and still be the wholly Other.

God is off the hook, so to say. We cannot really attribute our acts of virtue to God any more than we can attribute our acts of vice. They simply are not *God's* acts. Good acts are willed and done only by the powers gifted to us by God. By God's grace, as we say. God gifted us with the freedom to will and to do these acts, as perfectly responsible agents, as agents of true *self*-determination. God's graces of creation, both *ex nihilo* and *ex aliquo*, are more than sufficient for inspiring and sustaining our acts of freedom.

It is reprehensible on our part to attribute our acts of *vice* to God as their ultimate cause or condition. It is likewise wrong, moreover, to attribute our acts of *virtue* to God. God is the supreme, essential and necessary, grace for our very being, as well as for our acts of knowing and loving, and the rest. But God is *not* their doer, their free agent.

So, God is not at all responsible for the occupants in hell. And, in some way, God is not entirely *responsible* for the occupants of heaven. The fully free consent of the redeemed person is also *required*. God is gifter of the graces needed to arrive there; but these graces can be, and often are, freely refused. God does not specifically cause the refusal; otherwise, God would be saying *yes* and *no* simultaneously regarding the same thing. Paradox, but not contradiction, is an aspect of God's activity among us.

If God is not the supreme cause of evil—the supreme agent of why the deprived condition of will is there in our souls—then who or what is?

We are. Specifically, we are able to deny our freedom and to act against it. We are the only ones who can *determine ourselves* to be good-willing or evil-willing. Not God, not Lucifer, not friends and neighbors who support us or tempt us. Only we can and do elicit from ourselves acts of freedom or of denial of freedom that result in good or bad things happening to self and others. Only we can *self-determine*.

Other created persons can guide or misguide. These agents of influence may be human, angelic, or demonic. They can assist in the choice and execution of the act; but they cannot *do* the act.

God, of three uncreated Persons, provides *infinitely good* guidance. Yet the created agent can still exercise his or her freedom badly in the face of infinite goodness and power. Divine Power is infinite power-*with*, *not* power-*over*—

ineffably demonstrated by the passion and death of Jesus Christ.

We are able to decide fully whether an action of good or bad should be done. If, however, we are overwhelmed in our ability to decide freely, then the act is not one of freedom and moral responsibility on our part. But, insofar as there is even a slight measure of such ability (freedom) present, then to that slight extent we are *specifically* responsible, for the goodness of a good act or for the badness of a bad act.

A World of Supreme Meaning

Each person is a world of supreme meaning for himself or herself. The person will live with his or her ultimate self-determination and its meaning forever. The person can choose or *will* to let his or her meaning be the originally God-gifted one or to try to get meaning from some other source, namely, the self. For finite, fallible, and defectible creatures like us, so often the meaning for *being* starts, like the word *meaning*, with "me" instead of with God.

When a finite person elects to act, there is only one *decisive* source for the meaning of the act: that person himself or herself. The meaning is what the person either lets or gets. The person either tries to *let* the meaning for activity be what the Creator intended or tries to *get* meaning that is adverse and prompted by selfish desire.

In either case, the person creates, within his or her being, a world of received-meaning that helps to determine the "quality of life" not just for now, but forever. The world of a Satanic minion is not the world of God, but of total selfishness and masochism. The world of a good angel is the world of God, which that luminous person willed from the beginning of individual and communal creation *ex nihilo.*

But the world of human persons who live on earth—past, present, and future—is problematic. Such persons are in the process of making their final moves, either *of freedom-for-freedom* or *of "freedom"-for-denial*—denial with respect to the meaning with which they were first gifted totally by God.

There must be a supreme or ruling activity in each one of us whereby *we* determine what kind of meaning we will *receive.* All of our individual acts of freedom for good or ill must be symptoms or "creatures" of this supremely self-determining activity—the activity of our *agent will.*

In the world of meaning, there must be a supreme cause of virtue and vice that is not caused by any being other than ourselves—caused not by God, nor by any others. If we do not think so, then we are forced to conceive of ourselves as *ultimately* puppets of God, as it were, and we are verging on the threshold of a perhaps Manichean-like view, according to which we are tossed about by the competitive pulling of our strings, mere tools of the God of good and the God of evil.

There must be a supreme cause of good and evil *in* each one of us, the source of all of our acts, good and bad, virtuous and sinful. The reality of this personal world of meaning is analogous to the universal, common world of meaning for all created being. We are *like* God, who is the Creator of all being that is other than God.

We are not the creators *ex nihilo of our own being and agency.* God is. But we are *creators,* by our own *being,* of all of our acts of *doing*—including the doing of our *receiving*—*ex aliquo, out of our own gifted-being.*

So, we might do well to discuss the analogy for our own world of meaning: how our individual world of meaning is created *by our being* similar to the way God creates us, and how our destiny is *self*-determined: *how we are caused causes of happenings in our lives, while being uncaused causes of our own moral acts.*

First, it might be helpful to review how we can be sure that our being-at-all has an ultimate source of meaning: the Being of God.

The Uncaused Cause of Created Being

The classical manner of concluding to the reality of the Being of God follows a common pattern. We argue rather naturally *from* the reality of things or beings that are not self-explanatory *to* the unseen, yet knowable, reality of a being that is explanatory of all else and in no need of explanation. We call *God* the explanationless explanation of all else. *God is the uncaused cause: the cause that causes realities without its being caused in any way.*

In the historically celebrated ways of arguing for the reality of God, we often hear, for instance, about an unmoved mover, an uncaused cause, an absolutely necessary being, and the like. The manner of reasoning is similar.

It can go something like this. There are all about us in everyday experience, things in motion. And every one of them moves something else *only* insofar as it is *being moved* by other things. For instance, a cat bends the paper it walks on because life sources are affecting the animal, such as the heat of the sun and the nourishment it has ingested. The bent paper touches the sleeping baby's cheek and awakens the child because the cat happens to bend the paper to that extent. The whole world itself is full of moved movers and caused causes.

But these moved movers that we know about so readily, including ourselves, do not themselves explain why *they* are *at all*, what they *are* in themselves, and why they *move at all*.

We can analyze a *series* of moved movers, each of which moves something *only* to the extent that it itself is moved by something else. But there is *no basic (adequate) explanation in any* of the movers, nor in the whole series itself, for any given motion. When we consider the series itself, we have to conclude that, even if the series of such movers were supposedly *infinite*, that would not explain *what is happening right now in front of us*.

Why is the paper *moving at all*, and touching the baby's face? Why is there really occurring in front of us the very movement that we are trying to give a basic explanation for—why is the moving actually *being* or occurring at all?

Each of the *moved* movers is of *zero* value in explaining its *own* motion and also its causing of something else. No matter how many other moving things it itself is causing to move, it does *its* causing *only insofar* as it *is* moved or caused by another or others. And the same can be said about every mover in the series; it itself *explains nothing* about *why* the movement observed is *happening at all*. Zero value of explanation plus zero value of explanation, and so on, even if the series could be "infinite," would equal *zero* explanation for the motions and causations involved, including most critically the one we are directly observing.

Such moved movers and caused causes explain partly, perhaps, why the motions are of such and such a character: why the motions are so fast or slow, why they are happening now and not later, why they have various qualities and consequences. But the very *existence* or *being* of any given moved mover or of the whole series itself is *entirely unexplained*. And it is definitely *that* for which we want to receive an explanation. We want to know (among many other things) *why* this or that motion or causation is *actually* occurring. For that matter, why is not everything dead and still?

Only one reasonable conclusion can be made. There must be a being, independent of the series—however long or short the lineup may be—that moves or causes everything in the series, as well as the series as a whole, without itself being moved or caused. It is an *unmoved* mover of all else. Or an uncaused cause of all else. If we do not admit *that* conclusion we violate our basic power to reason and we thus prefer to hold that no movement can be explained as to *why* it occurs. (We insist, e.g., on an empirical explanation for the motion or effect in question, not an ontological one—not one of *being.*) Nihilism is an (irrational) "option."

The activity here and now of a prime mover that moves without itself being moved—that causes without itself being caused—is thereby known by any open-minded, receptive thinker. We know *that* an uncaused cause really *is* and is active here and now, moving or causing, supremely and ultimately, all being and activity within us and around us and far from us. All other, lesser movements, however microscopic or macroscopic they may be, are effects ultimately—and really immediately—of that grand "moving" or causing or necessitating activity of the unmoved mover, the uncaused cause, the necessitating agent.

Considering any given movement or effect in our environment or within ourselves, we can reason to the conclusion that it could not be happening *here and now* without some absolutely unique causation responsible for its happening-at-all, whatever the number and kind and variety of other movers and causes there might be that have a part in the total effect. If we are going to *respect our reason* we are going to conclude as much.

The ultimate and immediate cause of here-and-now motions and actions within us and around us we call *God*. Without special revelation, we can know *that* such a being really is and is acting, even though we do not know much about what this being is really like and *how* this being does the supreme, universal causing. But knowing *that it is so* is a first and most crucial step in healthy reasoning.

The Uncaused Cause of Self-Determining Effects

We can turn now to another quest for an uncaused cause: the uncaused cause of self-determining *effects*. This cause is *not* the uncaused cause of the *beings* that are self-determining. God is *that* cause. Self-determining creatures do not cause their own *being* to *be*.

Who or what is the uncaused cause of our own free decisions and actions in regard to their specific effects? *God is not*. We are. God is the cause of the being-at-all of ourselves and of our perfect freedom of essence and of much else, but God *cannot be* the cause of the choices that *we* are *gifted* by God to make. God is not a supreme, albeit subtle, puppeteer.

God gifts us with the power to choose. But we are the one *doing* the choosing activity. We *do* the choice by the way in which we receive the power to choose. God is, so to say, the gifter of the *power* to do, but we are the *doer* of the power-gift. Indeed, God gifts us with the power to *be* the doer, but we are the agent, the *doer* of the doing, determining its character as good or bad.

We need to distinguish, without separating, the *being* of the choice from the *doing* of it. We are *doing* the being of the choice, even as we are *receiving* the being of the choice and its power from God. In that way, we can say, we receive from God the choice that we are causing.

God is not receiving it as a doer of it, nor doing it. We are. But God is causing us to act with the freedom-power and with the *being-gifted* of the choice. We are being-gifted with the being of the choice, but not with its content. *We* are determining *that*.

God is causing us to do our own choosing in this self-determining act. Our choosing could not transpire without *both* God *and* us. Our self-determining act is a *co*-active reality, even as the act of *being*-created was a *co*-act of God and of us: we were receiving the act of being-created while doing it. (The act of being-created is not the same as God's act of creating. It is *our* act of *receiving* the *being* of our creation.)

Similarly, all of our acts of will that are free volitions participate in the primal activity of our being: receiving self while doing self—being gifted with self, while receiving and doing the being of self. By slurring over this distinction, we passively act or react.

In the preceding section of this Chapter, we have made a basic reflection on the *whole* of created *being* in showing the necessary Being of God. So, similarly, we can reflect on the whole being of any given person (particularly a human person) in showing the necessary self-determination of this creature.

We can start reflecting on any particular activity of self-determination and know that there is within it an ultimate or decisive source for all the specifically moral good and bad that emanates from it. There is a specifically God-like power within us that ultimately and specifically effects our personal destiny. Each human being is a microcosm, as it were, of the whole universe of created persons—angelic and human.

The New Reasoning

Let us examine, then, the personal relationships of human beings with respect to their own variously free activities that issue in *morally* good and bad effects. These activities are ones for which finite persons are specifically, if not totally, responsible. These acts are conditioned. They are helped or hindered by past parental influence, by the attitudes and behaviors of peers and role models, and by much conditioning from the physical and cultural milieu.

Most critically, these *personally responsible* acts are "infinitely conditioned" by God. But they are *not* acts of God or of any other being. They are acts *only* of the unique self. They are emanating from the person who is, of course, *acting uniquely* in the context of the actions of multitudes of other persons.

We can consider a person's morally significant activities, say, a decision on whether or whom to marry, on whether to pay income tax or go to jail, on whether to lie or tell the truth to someone who has a right to know, and the like. About each of such acts of decision-making, we can ask: Is this act—*of the person by the person*—uncaused?

No, the person himself or herself is the agent or effective *cause*. The act itself constitutes and causes the person's goodness or badness in behavior and personality. But the unique person is the *cause* of the act and of its inherent effects. So, this morally significant *act* is a *caused cause.*

Nonetheless, with respect to the particular moral good or bad—or good *and* bad—the *person* is the *uncaused cause* of the act and its morally significant effects. The act does not act. The *person* acts and causes.

We ask, for instance, the question about one of our own morally good or bad acts. And when reason tells us that this freely chosen act is ultimately caused by our free will—and not by the free will of God or that of our peers or that of anyone else—we can begin to regard our *will* as the common key area for responsibility.

Our will, however, is not responsible as such, *since the will is not the agent* (the *do*er), but is the *power* of the agent *by which* the agent—the responsible doer of the action—effects some good or evil.

So, just as the intellect or the mind does not know anything—that is, does not *do* the knowing, but is the *power by which* the knower knows—so, the will does not love or desire anything—that is, does not do the loving, but is the *power by which* the lover loves.

St. Thomas said it well: *hic homo intelligit.* This singular, whole person *knows.* And, we might add, the singular, whole person *loves.* The intellect does not know anything. The will does not love anyone. The particular person knows and loves *by* the powers of intellect and will.

Then, we can ask, "Is there not within each person an act that he or she is doing even now—a kind of non-effect cause (or "uncaused cause") for *all* of the particular good and the particular bad that the person does, whether consistently or in spurts?

Such an act would be the act of *be*-ing this person. Each of us is *doing* our *be*-ing, as well as other acts, such as liv-ing, walk-ing, talk-ing, know-ing, desir-ing and so forth. These latter are branch acts of the primal root-act of *be*-ing.

We must remember that we are not God—nor God, we—and so God cannot *do* our being and our choices for us and yet be God. Nor could we then be ourselves.

Yes, out of nothing, God gifts us with our power to will. But only we *do* the willing: by acting *with* this gift. God does not make the *willing* (choices) for us, and *could* not do so. And it is precisely because God is *infinitely* powerful that God *could not* do these free, *finite* willings, but super-generously *gifts* them through the powers of our gifted nature. God is not an insecure giver or gifter of being. God says, "Be," and we *are* fully forever.

We are not *pawns* of God, of our parents, or of our friends. We are essentially *free agents*. Much of the time, of course, our freedom is operating at relatively low ebb, and we are being highly conditioned by environmental forces. Perhaps we are not even *functioning* freely at all. But even then we are still *naturally* free.

The point is that if *we* do at least some volitional activity that is at least partly self-determining, and not totally the product of forces other than ourselves, then we are morally free *to that degree*. But any given act of free volition is of zero value in explaining *why* the act *is* and is *the way it is*: essentially a morally responsive activity.

None of our individual acts of volition in this life are isolated within us. They all must be emanating from a single directive source that we *are*. The directive source cannot be God, if these acts are our acts. And they definitely are. *We* are the director.

So, there must be a self-explaining act of willing and power to will (agent will) *by which* we do our variously individual acts of goodness and badness. None of the latter individual acts have any ultimate meaning for us, unless we give them ultimate meaning—for better or for worse—by a supremely causative power of self-destiny that sustains them.

Any given *act* of ours, good or bad, *as chosen or as a self-determination*, can be explained basically only by admitting a deep, core activity, a primary God-*like* one. This essentially abiding activity cannot be explained by anything other than its being an uncaused causing that *we* do. Any other activity of ours, whether of an emotional or physical or even intellective character, is of zero value in explaining the character of the core activity.

There must be, therefore, an activity of will—of *agent* will—that is totally an act of personal responsibility, radiating into all of our individual acts of responsibility, making them to be *ours* and to *be what they are as self-determining*, as moral, as contributing-to-destiny.

This core activity is the heart of personal responsibility. It is why we can *be* in heaven or *be* in hell. *We* are the only *decisive* cause of our being-there; and, in *this* respect, we are *not caused* or *conditioned* by any other. No one else is to be specifically credited or blamed.

God is the uncaused cause of our *whole being*. But *we* (as this whole person) are the uncaused cause of all of *our free behavior and attitudes*. Our *agent will*—the power of pure active potency to love—makes this possible. And we are exercising it now, for better or for worse, at a largely unconscious level of being.

In being this kind of uncaused cause, we are *not at all* the cause of our own *being* and of our *ability* to act—even to act freely. But we *are* the uncaused cause of the *act of receiving* our being from God, and that receiving is an *act of receiving* our *being-gifted by God out of nothing.* God's radically free gift-act of creating us out of nothing is quite other than *our act of receiving this being-gift.*[33]

Every simple volitional act of helping our neighbor to cross the street or to get through a heartbreaking event is a good act of ours that proceeds from virtue or a stable disposition to do good; and that disposition is developed and maintained by a certain degree of what we can call "good will" that is ours—not God's—at the inmost core of our being. How well are we even now *receiving* our act of being *as ours*, as well as receiving the being of others *as theirs*, including the Being of God *as God's*?

Who we will-to-be at root, causes the fruit. The good effects are caused by good habits established by earlier acts; but all acts and habits and attitudes are being caused *not by themselves*, but by that *supreme causal activity of freedom within us*, by which we determine the *kind* of human and individual person we are and will be. We ourselves are the *uncaused cause* of this determinative activity.

Our moral effects, good as well as bad, are caused by us. Past irresponsibility and actions of deviance build up a habit of ill-disposition. All bad acts and habits cannot be said to be isolated and totally disconnected features of our

---

[33] Our first act of receiving the being-gift that we are—this first act of our freedom—must have been done defectively and is necessarily hampering us in everything we think, say, and do.

being. They are *caused causes* of the bad. They emanate from ill-will, instigated at or near the center of our being—in our agent will. And no matter how they are inter-laced and interactive with other agents and with our own and others' good dispositions and influences, we are ultimately the uncaused cause of these acts and habits. We are the uncaused cause of the evil we do, by commission or by reception, as well as of the good we execute or receive.

If bad acts and habits did not proceed *from such an ultimate pivot*, we would not be free beings and responsible for acts and habits; we would be beings highly conditioned by our environment and *nothing more*. We could no more be punished by jail or fine or ostracization than could an errantly behaving monkey or rhinoceros.

Both good and bad proceed from the heart of the human agent, even though we cannot see this process "up close" in our own regard, let alone observe immediately such emanation from others. But we *know it must be so*.

Just as there cannot be an infinite series of "caused causes" of finite being in the universe of larger reality, so there cannot be an infinite series of "caused causes" of finite responsible behavior in the personal being of an individual agent.

Each act or habit of the individual person is of zero value in explaining *why* this person is doing or being this way or is developing this particular character. This act or that habit is, and is what it is, of and for the person, only insofar as it is caused by other acts or habits of the same person.

But postulating an "infinite" series of such acts or habits within the person regards the person as an "infinite being," which he or she is obviously not. Therefore, there must be a *first* or supreme *act* of the person *whereby* he or she is totally responsible for whatever he or she does or wills freely or for whatever he or she is, by free exercise, disposed to do. Contrary perhaps to ordinary perception, every created person is the uncaused cause of his or her moral good and moral evil.

We are the only agents to whom our actions that are good or bad, virtuous or vicious, can be attributed. We are able to respond (response-able) freely to one degree or another, and to that degree we are acting functionally as persons, not as things—even when we treat ourselves by such acts as though *we* were things.

We are the uncaused cause of moral good and evil in our lives. And, flowing from this determination, we cause the good and evil, specifically in our emotional, physical, and spiritual lives. We are not the uncaused cause of our *being* and of our being magnificent creatures of God. But we are the uncaused cause of *being here*, in need of God for redemption unto a new participation in our originative, perfect creation.

Chapter 16

Creation: Encounter of Two Perfect Freedoms

God initially gifts all created persons—angelic and human—with the integrity and freedom of *being their own beings*. God does not create marionettes of divine entertainment. We *are* fully our *own* being—not even partly God's being.

We do not merely *have* our being. We *are* our being. And we do *fully* our own acts, though they are now fraught with dependency on God in our doing of them. To think that they were *intended* to be *dependent originatively* is to treat God as a "high class creature," not as the infinitely good and powerful Creator of a perfect and immaculate creation.

We did not kill—nor could we kill—our *essential* relationship with God. Even in grievous sinfulness, we still are—as gifted originatively with being—independent with respect to God. But the originative, *super-relational* good of our independence-*with*-God has been profoundly distorted.

We remain even now independent-*with* God as gifted to be by God. We are, however, *also* somewhat independent *from* God, by having imperfectly received the gift of our being. The independence-*from* should not be thought to be a change *of* our God-gifted independence-*with*. Rather, it is a deformed receptedness that is self-demeaning. We are thus both perfect and imperfect persons. Perfect by virtue of God's irrevocable gift and by the degree of *yes* in our *maybe*; and imperfect by means of the *no* in that same response.

With this flawed condition of *being*, we are still capable of virtue, as well as of sin. Original sin is taken away at baptism, along with *originative* sin. But the profound effects remain.[34]

---

[34] Do we get in this life what we deserve from the particular way in which, or the degree to which, we sinned originatively? Yes, of course. But also more: based on how well or badly we conduct ourselves here and now in the course of our existential lives. We can mitigate much by the degree and character of our repentance. If we do not "come clean" at the moment of death, we cannot enter everlasting bliss.

The doctrine of purgatory is instructive here. All who enter heaven must do so in absolute purity—as the pure acts of be-ing that they were gifted to be. Their passive potency must be completely purged and transformed. God's redemptive Love made it possible for us to become converted to the core. But we must do our finite best, from the heart of our *be*-ing, to affirm this great gift.

People who suffer from severe handicaps—physically, emotionally, mentally, spiritually—as they enter or live in this world are not necessarily greater originative sinners than those who appear whole and unblemished. The latter might have to suffer much greater pain and discomfort later in life or in purgatory than those with obvious defects.

The defective character created by originative sin, as manifest in this life, is not only "on the surface," but also is much weightier in the depths. As the direct result of the crash of our beings, we all have deep-seated, largely unobservable streaks of good and bad potential character. Being alive in this world, we are already well on our way to the potential for repentance. We are just waking up to how well off we are, relative to our originative, self-inflicted numbness and to how bad off we are, relative to what we must face. We are like dazed and maimed self-observers recovering at a crash site, trying to determine "what happened and what to do now."

Comparison over who sinned most heavily originatively is absurd and would indicate great misunderstanding of the reality. Charity toward the oppressed and homeless is urgent, if we are going to show true repentance for our own *originative* sin. Let someone who is sinless cast the first assessment.

We are not virtue-puppets, exclusivistically dependent on God's will. Nor are we counter-gods, exclusively independent-of or -from God.

We are both dependent and independent with respect to God. We depend totally on God for salvation from our collapsed condition, even as we remain independent in our ongoing and final decision whether or not to accept the salvation.[35] We *maybe*-sayers are the supreme agents of our own acts, for better or for worse—for being willingly *with* God or willingly *with-out* God.

This means that the moment of creation is the supreme encounter of two perfect freedoms: God's and ours, Gifter-freedom and gifted-freedom. *As freedoms, they are independent with respect to each other.* God's infinite freedom, gifting our finite freedom, creates a relationship that is in reality neither interdependent nor independent-to-dependent. This interface of pure freedoms is inter-*independent* in its very *being*, if it is to be ultimately *freedom* at all.

---

[35] The final decision is at death. Even for those persons who die as human embryos. When we "die the death," it is the whole person who dies. Death *happens to* the whole person and brings to that final point all the good and bad of his or her life. To the degree of *yes* and *no* at the first moment of creation (*ex nihilo*) is added whatever "merit" or "demerit" that life in space and time have wrought. The modification undergone by one's lifetime of activity can be immense. Perhaps considerable repentance has been effected, perhaps little or none. Even persons who claim Jesus as Savior will need to reveal how sincere they are. Then the final judgment by the Redeemer will be made with infinite justice and mercy—neither vindictive nor permissive.

In the light of their participation in this redemptive world, all persons will likely be given an opportunity, once and for all, to say, with their whole *be*-ing, a final *yes* or *no*. Those who *do* a complete *yes* will enter beatitude immediately and forever. Those who do a response that is (finally) *more yes than no* will be purified in purgatory. Those who fall short of an adequate *yes*—not genuinely sincere—will create for themselves everlasting frustration. And there are likely degrees of beatitude (heaven) and of decisive self-frustration (hell).

Not everyone who had said during life, "Jesus is my Savior," will be saved, but only those who meant it sincerely by their commitment to virtuous living.

Creation *ex nihilo* is the supreme kind of causality, gifting persons to be and be perfectly who they are. But ordinary cosmic causality is not *necessarily* creative. The meaning of being an *infinite* cause of anything is quite different—and has to be—from being a finite cause, not to say an *imperfect* finite cause. We must make quite apparent to our understanding the *infinite difference* in kind between the causing done by an uncreated being and that done by created beings—especially fallen ones.

The way of the finite, self-afflicted human person in knowing and in doing is virtually the opposite of the way of infinite Being and Doing. For us to know something in our damaged condition is to depend on *vital instruments*, such as the senses—external and internal—and the practical intellect with its inexorable laws of logic based on the absolute dependency of conclusions upon premises. But for the divine Being to know is to *be infinitely present within* the known. Instruments, including logical processes, do not fit infinity—*nor do they even fit perfect finitude.*

In our present condition, *knowing* something is similar to *making* something. Making something, or causing it to exist, necessarily involves rendering the artifact dependent on the maker. We instinctively tend to assume that God's causality is something similar.

God, however, is not a Maker of being—being cannot be made or fashioned. For the divine Being to cause someone to *be* is to render the created (person) *independent-with* the Creator, and not a dependent function of the divine. No functionality at all. Pure celebration.

Instead of recognizing this primal truth, our fallen human minds overlook the *perfect creation* and project onto God *solely* the kind of creation involved in a recovering world—the world of becoming. Only in the redemptive world of both material and spiritual becoming are there created persons *dependent-on*-God-*with-hope-for-recovery.*

Independence-*with* God, Our First and Lasting Home

In our present condition of alienation in being and of passive-reactive self-satisfaction, we are largely lost. We do not "remember" our true and everlasting home. We do not even think that we ever had an original home.

We know that the cosmos is not such a dwelling. But we have no decisive recall of our ever having been present even to the "gates" of our home at the moment of creation *ex nihilo*. We do not remember our *being there*, while *not entering*.

But it is not surprising that we do not remember, since memory is cued to time and temporal events. Our creation *out of nothing* was not temporal, either for God or for us. So it is inaccessible to memory, yet it is quite knowable if we are willing to reflect cohesively.

Even though we cannot strictly recall the moment of creation and even though our response must have been immediately and ontologically repressed, the truth is that we immediately and partially refused the gift of being-*with* God.

This originative act did transpire. But our presence now to *infinite intimacy* is exceptionally repressed.

Somewhat understandably, then, Plato, considered to be the archetypal philosopher of the Western world, regarded our apprehending universal forms or ideas in our earthly life as an obscure act of remembering—a kind of "homing" endeavor. He seemed to think that we are recalling our spiritual and intellective home, from which we fell.

Unfortunately, Plato was unaware of the critical meaning of *being*, of creation *ex nihilo*, and of sufficiently *personal freedom*. He thereby failed to see the *personal* continuity between the present world and the "past" world. He had little appreciation of our *personal responsibility* for being here, and for creating our passive condition by a radical, full, signature act of freedom at the moment of being created entirely out of nothing. His philosophy did not acknowledge explicitly either free will or sin.

Plato's Forms were pure, yet finite. They were dubiously divine, even as was Aristotle's Pure Act or immobile mover. God, however, *is infinite*—the unlimited kind of being by whose activity limited kinds of being *are*.

Past history barely reveals God's infinity. The true infinity of God is largely missing in our spiritual and intellectual lives—even in our theological lives. This "missing infinity" represents alienation from our *being-with* God. Only if God is truly infinite can we be *independent-with* both finite and infinite being.

As we now stand in our knowledge, our God is never "big enough." Unfortunately, God is conceived, practically speaking, as "bigger than anything else and better than everything else taken together." We continue to treat God as *ex-isting*. God is thought to *exist*, rather than simply to *be* and to be unlimitedly *with* us. God is still not being understood *as really without any limits at all*.

Instead of being "face to face" with God—as we were created to be immediately, fully, and freely—we are now "face to face" with an incredibly vast (if finite) chasm or void "within and without" that we effectively *caused* by our first act of knowingful willing—a protoconscious act of a supreme kind of conscious knowing.

In our profoundly unconscious shame, we have attempted to hide ourselves from God. We are like Adam and Eve in the Garden. Yet, in the vortex of *originative* sin, we became reality's intimate "spin machine." We are, therefore, almost totally inclined to wonder how and why *God* is hiding *from us*.

But where can infinite actuality hide? Nowhere. God can no more hide from us than create an "infinite confusion." And God does not play games.

We are the hiders. We are exercised in myriad ways of fleeing from God and from ourselves, and especially from our originative relationship. We are still seeking, and are reticent about finding, the infinity of God—*the infinity* of love, justice, mercy, and power. We need a renewed and deeper sense of repentance.

By acknowledging the depths of our self-inflicted alienation and desperate need, we can become eventually free and *fully intimate with the infinite God.* We can become faithful to our being, as the gift of a perfect creation.

"Be you perfect,

as also your heavenly Father is perfect."

Matt. **5:48**

...as you have been created to be.

Robert E. Joyce is *professor emeritus* of philosophy at St. John's University in Minnesota. He received a B.A. in philosophy from the University of St. Mary of the Lake, Mundelein, Illinois, 1957; an M.A. in philosophy from De Paul University, 1960; and a Ph.D. in philosophy from International College, 1978. Doctoral studies were also done at the University of Notre Dame, 1959-61, where he served with a Teaching Fellowship, 1959-61, and as instructor of philosophy, 1961-62. He has taught philosophy also at De Paul University, Loyola University, the College of St. Benedict, and at St. John's University, 1962-94. At St. John's he spent some years as Director of the Tri-College Honors Program and as Chair of the Philosophy Department.

Professor Joyce is the author of five books and numerous articles in scholarly and popular publications.

He and his wife, Mary, published the first pro-life paperback in the United States, *Let Us Be Born: The Inhumanity of Abortion* (Chicago: Franciscan Herald Press, 1970). In the same year, they also published an introduction to their philosophy of man and woman, *New Dynamics in Sexual Love: A Revolutionary Approach to Marriage and Celibacy* (Collegeville, Minnesota: St. John's University Press, 1970). Robert's doctoral dissertation was published in 1980 by the University of America Press. *Human Sexual Ecology: A Philosophy and Ethics of Man and Woman* has been used by several leaders in the natural family planning movement.

Robert and Mary Joyce reside in St. Cloud, Minnesota.

Glossary

Coming to Terms. The new theistic view requires an adventure in revisiting traditional terms. Faith and reason need an increase in depth-perspective on perennial truths.

Painters, for instance, once rendered their images in largely flat-seeming, two-dimensional presentations. They seemed not to know how to represent the third dimension. Similarly, because of a cosmological crunch, traditional philosophy and theology tend to be two-dimensional in presenting the great truths. If possible, our effort here is to change *not the truths, but the perspective* for the sake of better vision.

The following definitions and delineations of some key terms might assist the reader's thinking about prospects for a better theistic view. These words and phrases are analogical, not univocal. They do not have one single, exclusive meaning. For brevity and practicality, however, only one or two main meanings are set down for each term.

God is the infinite Being of three Persons, who gifted all created beings to *be*. God is not merely perfect, all-good, and all-powerful. God is *unlimitedly* so. God is not a "whole being," some kind of mega-creature; God is unlimitedly unique being.

Being and Becoming

Being (*ens*) can mean the totality of a given being: who and what it is. But, more specifically, be-ing (*esse*) is the *act*uality of being-at-all. Be-ing is the most important *act* of a whole being. All other acts and actualities, such as thinking, drinking, walking, talking, *et al*. are "branches of the act of be-ing." Somewhat counter to the traditional theism, being is regarded, in this book, as something we *are* and *do*. Be-ing is the gift God gives us to be and to *do*. *We* do our being. God does not. Being is an act, not merely a fact.

We do not simply "have" being. We *are* the entire be-ing God gifted us uniquely to *be* and to *do*. No part of our being is of God or of anyone else. We are fully and forever our own unique being, thanks to the *infinitely* powerful gifting of God.

Only persons are *whole* (complete) beings. Subpersonal beings (from molecules to monkeys) are *part* (incomplete) beings. They cannot receive themselves within themselves and so are not, and *cannot be, fully* what they are. (See *excidents*)

To *be* is to be *unique* (to be not the same as anything else) *and* to be *uniquely related* (to every other being that is). For person-beings, to *be* is (also) to *be-with*.

Existence is a *way* of being, of standing outside of self and other things. *Ex-sistere* means to "stand out of." But God and all created persons who said fully *yes* to creation *ex nihilo* do not *exist*; they simply *are*. They have no passivity to "overcome" by striving to get out of or beyond their condition of being.

All material beings, as we know them now, not only *are*, but *ex-ist*. Subpersonal beings exist by having "parts outside of parts," by being extended, material realities. Personal beings who, like us, have fallen—who are defective—*ex-ist* also by reflective consciousness, whereby they "stand outside" themselves by being conscious of themselves, the better to direct themselves and make choices (the existentialist aspect).

Failure to distinguish meaningfully between *being* and *existence* (in any language equivalent) can be seen as a particularly instructive sign of our originative repression of our *first* act of *be*-ing and of the ex-istence that this act caused.

The *pre-conceptive latency of our fallen being* (*ontological latency*) is the coma-like, disordered way of being from which we emerge at conception. It was caused immediately by the crash of saying *maybe* at the moment of creation *ex nihilo*.

This condition of collapsed being before existence (conception) has nothing to do with reincarnation or even incarnation. There was no "taking on" of any kind. The perfect (finite) ontological structure with which we were gifted at creation *ex nihilo* was compromised by our imperfect response. Immediately, we became imperfect created persons by way of *adding* an *imperfect receiving* to our originative perfection or giftedness. We became, as it were, "bloated in our being." Our perfect, God-gifted essence remained, but our nature—the disposition to act according to essence—was self-distorted.

Maybe-sayers thus subsist prior to their space-time ex-istence at conception. Our pre-conceptive latency is the condition of our being following the moment of *our imperfect response* to originative creation right up to the moment of conception. Our self-conflicted be-ing (including powers to know and love) was relatively dysfunctional until that event. We were not fallen angels, but simply fallen humans.

Energy is the natural capacity to do work: to struggle, strain, move forward, exercise potencies to do and to be done to. It arises from the fractuation (fractured actuation) done by the *maybe*-saying of originatively sinning persons and it comes in many forms at various levels of redemptive causality. Without any originative sin, there would be no need or occasion for energy. Every reality would be a *pure act* or *actuality*—whether infinite or finite. No work to be done. Simply, the play of everlasting life.

Essence is *what* someone or something *is*. While one can focus on the essences of qualities and activities of entities, the prime signification relates to the *fundamental what*: *what* is a person, *what* is this thing or that thing as such. Fundamentally, what *kind* of person or thing is this as different from other kinds of reality?

But there are really two different—almost always confused—kinds of essence: *common* (e.g., human) and *individual* (e.g., *this* human). The confusion between, say, the humanness and Jamesness of James makes for much metaphysical mischief in giving an account of being *as being. What James is* as this unique human (his uniqueness of person) is not at all the same as his being a human kind of being.

Nature is the essence of someone or something as this essence is disposed to act. What kinds of activity can we expect from this or that entity? Granted the essence of a peach tree is to produce peaches—not apples, oranges, *et al.*—its nature is the inexorable disposition to do just that. The way the being expresses itself, or can express itself, in action is its nature. *Nature* is, so to say, *how* the essence can reveal itself in acting. In saying *yes, no,* or *maybe* to being and God, the *self acts through* its essence, but *in and by* its nature.

Form (substantial form), traditionally conceived, is that principle in the *essence* of a person or thing *by which* the entity is *fundamentally what* it is. It is an intrinsic *part* of the essence. All things have substantial forms: one for each kind of thing.

This traditional meaning is considerably modified by the theses of this book. In the new view, substantial form is the principle of the person (not of things) *by which* he or she is able to give self to self and to all others as a principle of essence. In the new view, it is called "givity": the capacity specifically to give in a receiving way. It is the principle that is co-active with matter and is a dimension of the *act* of *be*-ing. To be is to be giftive (and to be receptive).

In the new view, human souls are the substantial forms *as they serve* human persons in their recovering from defective exercise of "givity" at the moment of their originative creation and serve in their struggle to attain the pristine, God-intended condition of gifting selves fully at the moment of creation.

Matter (prime matter), traditionally conceived, is that principle in the *essence* of a human person or thing *out of which* the entity is *fundamentally what* it is. Matter is an intrinsic part of the essence. All things in matter and motion, space and time, involve prime matter, from which every diverse kind of thing is developed. It is the ultimately common feature of substances in the cosmos. None can exist without it. This traditional meaning is, however, considerably modified—not negated—by the theses of this book.

Prime matter (reconceived in the light of Faith and ontological reflection), first of all, is the principle of the human *person* (not of any *thing*) *by which* he or she is able to receive self from within self as a characteristic of essence. (Angels have no prime matter. Their kind of essence itself is pure receptivity to their be-ing.) (God's

Being is pure *infinite* receptivity, as well as infinite givity.) This pure receptivity-power, co-constitutive of the essence, was gifted at the moment of creation *ex nihilo*.

In the new view, matter is a kind of *receptivity*: the capacity to *receive* one's essence in a giving way—and not at all "to be done to" or "to be determined." The prime matter and substantial form are totally correlative as the roots of all receiving and giving in the human person from the moment of originative creation.

Originative matter was *purely* **active receptivity**—*the active power or potency to receive who and what* we are. It was not—originatively—the *passivity* or passive receptivity delineated by Aristotle.

Pure originative receiving is just as active and real as giving. *Originatively*, there is no passivity.

With our bad originative response, prime matter as sheer receptivity within our essence had to begin functioning as prime matter that is passive, a capacity to "be done to" right within the essence and to function in common with the extrinsic energy of subpersonal creation. Out of this passive condition, human bodies were formed. Our bodies are prime matter *as it serves* human persons in attempting to attain the pristine condition of receptivity intended by God at the moment of creation.

Angelic persons, however, in their greater simplicity and likeness to God's infinite receptivity, are without this co-principle within their essence. Originatively, angels are simple, sheer receptivities for the act of be-ing.

The following terms—except active potency—apply strictly to existents in the cosmos, not to angelic creatures.

Substance is, above all, like unto what Aristotle said it was in the first instance (primary substance): this whole being...its essence, with all its attributes and weaknesses, concretely and singly. More specifically, in accord with the common tradition, substance (second substance) is also that principle in the being of a person or thing *by which* the entity is or exists *in and through itself* and not in and through any other. Every created substance is its own principle of intrinsic being and activity (but not its own ultimate cause). It remains the source of natural stability in the midst of accident-modifications or changes. In space and time, substance relates to accidents as passive potency (*q.v.*), out of which qualities and acts develop.

Accidents are not the substance, but parts of the substance, through which the substance *manifests itself.* An accident, such as the color of a tree or the thought of a human, does not be or exist in and through itself, but only *in and through another* (a substance). The act of walking and even the power to walk, as instances, are accidents and cannot be or exist "on their own" or in and through themselves. There is no act of walking without a walker, nor act of thinking without a thinker. Yet the acts are real; they express or manifest the substance or agent and are never to be discounted—even if minor.

Excidents, according to the new view, are the super-multiplicity of substances and their accidents in the cosmos that are not *entitatively* human. Excidents are *everything in the whole of space and time*, including every particle of organic and inorganic matter—and excluding human substance (persons) with all their accidents. At the base of all excidents lies a supremely low level of human (non-entitative) fallen freedom empowering the telic character of all matter and motion. All material things tend, however erratically, to an end or fulfillment of inherent purpose by virtue of their being entities created by God out of fallen human freedom (energy).

At the moment of creation *ex nihilo, excidents* resulted from the ontological explosion caused by our immediate response. They are forms of the passive-reactivity (i.e., energy) emanating from the originative sin that was constituted by the first acts of innumerable humans who said *maybe* to be-ing. These elements of discarded human freedom were separated from the malreceptive, freedom-abusive sinning persons themselves. As subpersonal (partial) beings (molecules to monkeys), they were developed by God's *infinitely* loving activity of compassion on the *maybe*-sayers.

Energy originally emanated from the primal partial rejection (the fractuality) of the perfect personal beings that we were gifted to be. All energy is originatively human energy—frustrated human freedom—and is of two basic kinds: *fragmental* and *non-fragmental*. On the one hand, excidents are *fragmental* energy, "broken off" from the substance of the *maybe*-sayers in the ontological "big bang." On the other hand, fallen human substances retained a kind of *non-fragmental* energy that is therapeutic and intrinsic to them. The result is our defective substances with their accidents (including bodily life in the cosmos).

Active potency is the ability or capacity to *do* something or to *perform* a certain kind of activity. By creation *ex nihilo* we were gifted to *be* pure active potencies of be-ing—each person fully able both to receive and to give personal be-ing. After originative sin, fallen human being has the active (natural) capacity (whether functional or not) to reason and to love; a dog does not. A dog has the active potency to bark and wag its tail; a human does not. *Pure* active potency, however, is the kind of being we were gifted to be *out of nothing*. It was not mixed with any passive potency. We created the latter by our less-than-full response.

Passive potency is the ability or capacity to *be done to*, to *be affected by* or determined by someone else or something else. A tree has the capacity (passive potency) to be bent by the wind; a boulder does not. A boulder has the capacity (passive potency) to be rolled down a hill; a (living) tree does not.

Moreover, "prime matter" in the traditional sense is a sheerly passive receptivity—prime passive potency. In the new view, however, prime matter is *originatively* a supreme, purely active, receptivity of essence right within the essence—an *active potency*. God does *not*, and cannot, create *directly* out of nothing any passive potency.

As perfectly self-actuated, angels and saints in heaven are purely active potencies that co-act *with* God and the others, without being acted *upon* or determined in any way. There is no *passive* potency in beatitutde.

Creation

Creation *ex nihilo* (out of nothing) is the *originative beginning of all finite being*. God infinitely loved persons into being. Only persons resulted—out of nothing, out of no preceding substance. The creation was immediate, non-durational, and immaculate. Each person was unique and perfect in every way, including the freedom (purely active potency) to say *yes* fully. There was no temptation or ability to *be* tempted. Simply, there was gifted an invitation to *being with* God and all others 'ecstatically' forever.

This creation was perfectly *interpersonal* in divine intent and solely an act of God.

Creation *ex aliquo* (out of something) is the (*secondary* or *derivative*) creation of *be-coming*: being coming back to itself from a crash and from its ontological self-conflict. This remedial act of God began at the same moment as creation *ex nihilo* and our response. God "works with and out of" the results of the originative crash of those persons who said *maybe* to the gift of being in the *ex nihilo* creation. Infinite love and power interacts with finite, free resistance that is both conscious and unconscious.

This redemptive opportunity for salvation of these "fallen human persons" is what is directly the subject of the *Book of Genesis* and other Scriptures. According to Christian teaching, this redemptive creation of *becoming* culminated in the death and resurrectional life of Jesus Christ. At least, it can be said that, for all three theistic traditions, only God can redeem and save us.

While originative *creation* is interpersonal, but solely the act of God, *salvation* itself is an interpersonal act of finite freedom completely cooperating with infinite freedom.

Immaculate creation is another name for the interpersonal, immediate, durationless originative creation *ex nihilo* by which God gifted into being perfect persons with perfect freedom (as pure and unique acts of personhood, able to receive their being perfectly). The result of God's act of creating was beings unstained by any passivity at all. All gifted persons (angelic and human) were purely (immaculately) who and what they were by the power of the infinitely loving heart of God and necessarily gave their interpersonal response (*"yes, no,* or *maybe"*).

Freedom and Sin

Freedom is the correlative capacity of intellect and will to let the person be present to, and unite with, the Being of God *and* to participate in the fundamental goods of human personhood. Essence-freedom is structured to unite directly with—*not an identity with*—the essence of God, if or when beatitude is attained.

Natural freedom is, then, the *essential disposition* to know and to love, to the fullest extent of one's capacity of be-ing.

Functional freedom is the actual doing of the knowing and loving. Both natural and functional freedom are gifted in originative creation. But the defective response of our first act of freedom maimed them both, functionally separating them from each other and from the freedom of essence, the being as originatively gifted.

The alternatives of *yes, no,* or *maybe* were not set up "ahead of time." Our originative freedom was "pre-alternative." Before we broke out into the alternative conditions of being-and-becoming, we were *free*—like God—only to say *yes*. But being finite, we were *able* to say *no*. We were not *free* to say *no*; but we were *able* and did, *de facto—severely damaging our freedom.* Only then did arise the passively based kind of freedom with its alternatives and choices.

Originative sin is our *first maybe* (less than a full *yes*), said to God and ourselves with perfect, untempted freedom at the non-durational, immediate moment of creation *ex nihilo.* The degree of *no* in that *maybe* is not the only cause, but it is the ultimate cause, of all evil *in which we find ourselves involved.*

This primal sin caused our very exposure to the evils done by others—including the forces of Satan—as well as evils done by ourselves. Without originative sin we would be completely blissful in be-ing. By this abuse of perfect freedom we are now in the cosmic world of space and time—"all spaced out" and "doing time."

Original sin in Eden is a subject for *reportorial* Revelation. It is known by Faith in Scripture and Tradition. *Originative* sin, however, is a subject for our *personal* admission. It was not one of our temporal decisions or events, and thereby could not be readily "reported." But it can be *admitted* in the light of Revelation. This signature sin is received unconsciously by Faith in Scripture and

Tradition; and it is discerned, at least somewhat, by awareness of our being as *be*-ing—by beingfully (ontologically) received Faith.

Original sin is the first recorded historical sin. Adam and Eve committed this disobedience as they were tested through the serpent. God "predicted" it in saying that on the day you "eat of it (the forbidden fruit), you will die the death." This sin manifested to Adam and Eve their own weakness already present in the Garden of Eden as the result of their *ontologically* prior and repressed *originative* sin, committed along with all the rest of us. The *original* sin in Eden initiated the execution of the punishment of *originative* sin for all of us. It included our generation in the world of space and time, that made it possible for us to wake up to our sinfulness and our need for a Savior.

Knowing

Knowing is, quintessentially, a personal activity by which we are related intentionally to the being and essence of everyone and everything. It is proper to all persons. Every person is doing it, even if unconsciously. Despite our present degree of consciousness, therefore, knowing is also vastly unconscious for those of us in the fallen world. The largely repressed origin of unconscious knowing is our response in the moment of creation *ex nihilo*.

Starting from our present fixation on an implicit framework of space and time for everything, *we think that* conscious knowing in this world *initiates* the connection between knower and known, between ourselves and the world we are knowing. But the connection or "intactness" is already there—having been buried by our ontological repression.

Knowing in the spatiotemporal world, then, is remedial—a knowing derivative of the primal knowing, done by our being as be-ing. It is the tip of the iceberg.

We cannot not know, in some manner—however remotely and confusedly—all that is. To be is to know (finitely, for created persons) all that is, at least to some degree. God is known by everyone, whether consciously or unconsciously or partly both. So, too, is known everyone in creation, spiritual and temporal (past, present, and future). Unconscious, subconscious, and preconscious knowing are bases, out of which *conscious* knowing occurs.

Sensory knowing is also real, but peripheral, and not necessarily personal (i.e., as in animals). By sensation alone—whether internal or external—the essence of anything is never known.

We have been hardened perennially by the idea that there is nothing in the intellect that was not first in some manner in the senses. So, we instinctively think that substantial knowing is a kind of "gap jumping." By the power of its "intentionality" (other-directedness) and by the light of an "agent intellect," the ordinary (potential) intellect is thought to initiate contact with the essences of people and things (called "objects" of knowledge) by 'jumping the gap' between knowing power and known realities.

Such a knowing, however, is found only in redemptive creation (*ex aliquo*). This knowing is itself founded on the gapless and super-dynamic radiation of knowledge coming from the ever-nurturing originative knowing at the moment of creation *ex nihilo*. In that originative creation, we knew, *and still know, all that is*, by our *finite* powers of intellect and will, now so sorely abused. The common practice of identifying knowing as *solely within* our earthly predicament reinforces our originative repression and keeps us "locked out" of the depths of our be-ing and a much fuller meaning for who we are even at present.

The empirical and quasi-empirical dimensions of intellection here and now beg for support from the strictly non-empirical, but archetypally relevant dimensions. Wisdom is a loving kind of knowing and a knowing kind of love.

Conscious is the manner of knowing that we all desire now. As experienced in the present world, conscious knowing is necessarily narrow, focused, and precludes much. Nevertheless, before we know things consciously, we know them unconsciously, perhaps also subconsciously, definitely preconsciously, and above all, protoconsciously. Conscious knowledge and awareness of someone or something can come about in various ways (such as immediate intellection or intuition, instruction from another, recalling or memory, individual or collective probing and investigation, meditation, contemplation, and so forth).

Subconscious is the manner of knowing things that are just below the surface of consciousness. We are always knowing subconsciously particular things, many of which are semi-conscious, or at least partially conscious. Subconscious things often can be readily brought to consciousness. How to do ordinary tasks such as eating, washing dishes, playing tennis, playing the piano, and all manner of "automatic" activities constitute one major area of the subconscious.

Unconscious is the repressed manner of knowing persons, things, and meanings that are buried deeply away from conscious life. Much is rarely accessible to consciousness as formed in this world. But the whole of the unconscious plays its part in influencing thought and behavior. It is meaningful to distinguish the emotional or psychic unconscious (recognized psychoanalytically) from the spiritual and ontological unconscious, so prominent in this book.

We might even speak of the physical unconscious. It includes all human physiological and physical actions of which we are not conscious. Together, the physical, the psychic, and the spiritual unconscious—including the "collective and archetypal unconscious"—form a virtually horizonless ocean of potential meaning.

Some have represented the unconscious as featuring levels. Included are the subconscious, along with various kinds of deeply buried meaning.

From the ontological standpoint in this book, we know *protoconsciously* everything that is. Such knowledge was "smashed and packed down" by the sin forming our *unconsciousness*. Therefore, when we consciously know something in this world, especially new meanings, we do not simply come to know it "out of the blue." Rather, we come to *know that we know* it finitely, and with much inadequacy.

Preconscious (non-Freudian) is the manner of knowing persons and activities that are *spiritually unconscious*. Persons and activities that are critical to our being are particularly known in this way. The preconscious area of reality occurs prior to the development of ordinary consciousness. It is most directly beingful in its bearing upon us. This ontological level of knowing—in this book, the spiritually unconscious—is quite closely associated with our originative act of freedom in creation *ex nihilo*.

Protoconscious is the manner of knowing by which we originatively received our be-ing from God. It is our originative knowing of God, self, and all others at the non-durational, first moment of creation. This is the archetype of what we now know and call consciousness: our ordinary consciousness that is partial, functional, and privileged as redemptive.

Repression is the unconscious denial that we know some event, actuality, emotion, feeling, or value even as we *do know it unconsciously*. This mechanism of human knowing is an attempt to protect the knower from impulses, images, concepts, memories, meanings, and values that would likely cause anxiety and various disturbances. Repression is never good, but often inevitable.

The supreme instance of such "protection" is our immediate denial to ourselves of what we failed to do at the moment of being created out of nothing. This prime repression keeps us from recognizing our originative sin, the ultimate cause of *all* evil in our lives. It virtually requires blaming Adam, Eve, the serpent, and God for originating our predicament.

Psychoanalytic repression—repression of unwanted emotional and mental content—is better known at present and to be taken seriously; but it does not even get near to the root of our spiritual denial of originative sin. The latter is the supreme reason for all repression and suppression.

Suppression is the *conscious* attempt to be unaware of, or not to attend to, the multiplicity of events, actualities, emotions, feelings, or values that flood our everyday lives. Generally, it is a good and necessary endeavor that is ongoing and allows us to concentrate on one thing at a time. Often it is an explicitly deliberate attempt to block awareness of something undesirable. This activity can be good or bad, depending on the issue at hand.

Suppression is a conscious activity, even if quick and minimally explicit. Repression, however, is always an unconscious activity.

Intellect

In the new view, intellect and will are co-dimensions of the *be-ing* that each created person *is*. They are the "know and love" powers of *be-ing*. To be, for a person, is to *know* and to *will*. It is impossible for a person to *be* without also knowing and willing *protoconsciously*—however well or poorly.

Intellect and will are more than simply faculties of reparative and recuperative action in the world of be-coming, as we first come to be aware of them. They *are* the created being as knowing and willing (loving or hating) originatively and forever.

Potential Intellect is the power to know *by which* we are in touch with, and called to become wedded to, the essence and being of everyone and everything good.

In our common earthly life, this power does the conceiving, judging, and reasoning. It operates in being determined ("stimulated") by the objects of knowledge. It is the ability to be-done-to by whatever it conceives. It is ecstatically fulfilled in heaven, and is an instrument of supreme self-torture in hell.

Agent intellect, in traditional thought from Aristotle onward, is a pure act of intelligibility-giving. It is characterized as a supreme light that renders what is potentially knowable by the potential intellect actually knowable. It is a supreme instrument of knowledge, without itself being a knowing power.

In the new view, however, agent intellect is the originative capacity to *know* (fully and directly)(a purely active power to know)—to be united with all persons, infinite and finite, in their being and essence. It is the only way *knowing* transpires in heaven.

Will

Potential Will is the power, in space and time, to love *by which* we affirm, and are called to unite with, the essence and being of everyone and everything good. The objects of the will determine or "act upon" it in the holistic processes such as loving, desiring, delighting, being repelled, and the like. Thus will functions in the redemptive creation as a critical means of coming to what God has prepared for those who would love forever.

Agent Will is the power to love, to say *fully yes* to God, self, and others immediately and forever—right from the originative beginning. From "moment one" in creation, we did not fully exercise it. This power is now almost totally repressed.

In classical philosophy, the missing elements are curious concerning the agent (active) intellect and the agent (active) will. The agent intellect is portrayed as not knowing anything. And the notion of an agent will is virtually non-existent. But one cannot reasonably conceive of intellect without a corresponding will, and *vice versa*. That idea has been axiomatic in terms of the traditional understanding of potential intellect and potential will. Such can be no less true for active intellect and active will.

It is interesting to realize that the classical tradition recognizes, from the thought of Aristotle, the reality of an agent (purely active) *intellect*. But it fails to acknowledge it as *both* a light *and* a purely receptive knowing power for executing a pure act of knowing.

Nowhere, however, do we find acknowledgement of a truly agent (purely active) *will* by which we committed our personal originative sin, but could have instead related perfectly with God forever.

At the heart of all knowing and loving, **agent intellect** is our purely active power of emphatically receiving ourselves and others, even as **agent will** is our purely active power of emphatically *gifting* to ourselves and others. In hell, **agent will** represses itself so severely that one can blame all adversity on God. In heaven, **agent will** is our central loving power, uniting us with God in utter bliss forever.

Agent intellect and agent will have been largely passivized (contaminated) by their originatively defective activity. Every passive condition of intellection and of volition requires, as its base, a purely active agency, as gifted by God at the core of one's being. Only by agent will, for instance, can we love God with our "whole mind and heart."

Loving

Loving is willing the truest and best for self and *all* others, despite the cost. Not wanting or wishing, but *willing*. Our loving comes in degrees of intensity. At any given time, however, we love everyone, including God, with the same intensity. Often confused with liking, loving has nothing *essentially* to do with pleasure and pain. Love of enemies and of friends is the call to all that they may live well the be-ing with which they were originatively gifted.

At any given moment, we love everyone with the same *intensity*, but we know and love some persons with much greater *richness* than with others, based on our mutual experience, affection, and value sharing. If we were to consider whom we *love* least in this world: we can know that *that* is how *intensely* we love God, all others, and ourselves.

Affirmational love (see *loving*) is the central form of at least five kinds of love. Affirmation is the attitude of spontaneously delighting in another person and giving the other to himself or herself in an unqualified manner. The beloved feels loved and gifted as good unconditionally by the lover. Obviously, God is the supreme Gifter of being: of gifting to another (the created person) his or her whole being, without any "strings" attached.

Traditionally, *storge, eros, philia,* and *agape* are often cited. In general, they are forms either of giving others to self (such as *eros*) or of giving self to others (such as *agape*).

None of these, however, express the central meaning of love found in *originative creation*. And when created persons come to realize *existentially* how they have been gifted by God, they are much better able to "pass it on" in attitude and in deed to their companions in being. God's act of creating was an *infinite willing* of each of us to *be*, to be this unique person, and to *be-with* God—literally giving us to ourselves to *be* forever.

Friendship is a relationship that is of genuine love (see above) in which the persons share some sense of equality and esteem, including affection, and an ever-increasing participation in common values. The depth of the friendship can be assessed by the degree to which the friends participate in the most fundamental, spiritual values of human life. We *love* our friends more richly than others, but not more intensely.

In brief, friendship is loving plus liking. It is distinguishable from "enemyship," that is, loving plus disliking.

Assorted Terms

Experience is the conscious participation in the world of space and time. It is essentially a *felt being-done-to*. It can be pleasant or unpleasant, happy or unhappy by virtue of how one's consciousness is affected by the interaction with others and the movements of the self.

Experience is a bit like the wrapping or insulation on an electric wire. It can serve as a protection from what is really going on, what is going through the wire. Or it can be stripped away…by death. Experience is the conscious impact upon us of the world of passive potency.

But our activities or acts that the experience surrounds are independent of the "wrapping" or experience. We inveterately fail to identify the difference between acting and being acted upon while acting, even as we fail to identify the difference between being and existence. Ex-perience happens only in ex-istence and in our outsideness kind of agency. Every experience—including the mystical—"hides" an act or acting that is at least a little bit other than the experience itself, even as every existent—being that ex-ists—hides the act that is the be-ing of it all….However positive our experience is, it is basically passive (passive-reactive in the ontological sense).

There is no experience in heaven. No beatific *experience*. Just sheerly ecstatic, egoless participation in the Being of God and of one another—incomparably more joyful than any *experience*. The heart of acting and co-acting is passivity-free, existence-free, and experience-free. All is be-ing and lov-ing in consummate joy.

Experience provides opportunity for learning here in creation *ex aliquo*. But experience is not "the best teacher." It is not a teacher at all. The one who experiences teaches self or is taught *through* experience, not *by* it.

Perfection is a term that literally suggests the fulfillment of a process, a making (*per-facere*, to make through and through). Nevertheless, traditionally, it seems to be purged of any suggestion of process as when it is applied to God and angels. For the most part, it means *flawless, without blemish or defect.*

The scholastic philosophers and theologians made much of a distinction between what they called pure and mixed perfections. Pure perfections are those attributes such as intellect, knowledge, love, truth, *et al.* that do not necessarily suggest any passivity or "limitation." Mixed perfections are those qualities that necessarily are a mix of actuality and passive potency, such as colors, sounds, bodies, *et al.*

In the new view, these perspectives on perfection are included, but a new and critical emphasis is placed on the difference between perfection (flawlessness) that is *finite*, including the immediate *effects* of the divine Creator's action, and perfection that is *infinite* (God).

Created goodness, for instance, is not fulfilled in infinite Goodness, but in its own kind of *finite* gifted *perfection.*

We are fulfilled *by* God—and by our cooperative selves. But God is not our fullness. This fullness is ever finite and perfect. Infinite goodness is the only ultimate *cause* of our complete fulfillment, not the fulfillment or perfection itself.

Conception (human) is our individual entry into the cosmos. Prior to conception we were redeemable, but we were almost entirely dysfunctional. Conception is not the beginning of the person's *being*, but the *beginning* of the *becoming* (positive growth and awareness)—the person's coming back, within God's redeeming action, to a condition of originatively-intended *being*. Conception *happens to* the person and initiates formal participation in the spatiotemporal dimension of redemptive activity.

Death is the exit of a redeemed person from the opportunities of the awakening, alerting life in the cosmos. It is entry into everlasting destiny, through divine judgment—into heaven, hell, or final purgation for heaven. What is left in space and time are the *remains* of that person's cosmic participation. The corpse is not the body itself, but "exhaust" from the person's dynamic thrust through space and time.

The internal or spiritual body by which the earthly participation was specifically effected goes with the person and is not separated from the soul. What is separated is the person's empirical (placenta-like) connectedness with life in cosmic matter.

The soul and ontological body are reparative dimensions of the originative form (givity) and matter (receptivity) of the person. They could not separate from each other, without loss of *essential ontological integrity*. In hell, they are "impossibly united" as essential parts and are inexorably at war with each other forever. In heaven, they are "radiantly harmonious" with each other forever.

Grace is the infinitely affirming Being of God as gifting us with the union of love and perfect friendship. The grace of creation—being brought to be "out of nothing" in an unlimitedly unconditional way—is the supreme gift that we failed to receive *fully*. The grace of redemption and of salvation is the same open union of love offered to us in myriad ways throughout our lives and correlates with the grace of sanctification.

Reading Available from *LifeCom* in the **Two Creations Series**

Affirming Our Freedom in God:
The Untold Story of Creation
(LifeCom, 2001) 100 pages.

The Cry of Why beneath the Holocaust; Are We Hiding Something? God Freely Creates Our Freedom to Create, *et al.*

Facing the Dark Side of Genesis:
A New Understanding of Ourselves
(LifeCom, 2008) 84 pages, including Glossary

The Genesis Gap; Originative Sin; Theology of the Person's Being; Two Creations: Originative and Redemptive; Consequences for a Life of Faith, *et al.*

A Perfect Creation:
The Light behind the Dark Side of Genesis
(LifeCom, 2008) 170 pages, including Glossary

From Chaos to Cosmos; The Missing Infinity of God; God's Intimate Act of Creation; The Meaning of Evil and Its Cause, *et al.*

The following comprehensive volume may be pre-ordered:

When God Said Be, We Said Maybe:
An Inside Story of the Creation, the Crash, and the Recovery
(LifeCom, 2009) 480 pages, including Glossary

Booklets:

The Origin of Pain and Evil
(LifeCom, 2008) 40 pages

The Immaculate Conception: An Inside Story
(LifeCom, 2008) 20 pages

LifeCom
Box 1832, St. Cloud, MN 56302
www.Lifemeaning.com

www.ingramcontent.com/pod-product-compliance
Lightning Source LLC
Chambersburg PA
CBHW031300090426
42742CB00007B/534